# COLOURFUL CONTAINERS

CLB 4528
This edition published 1995 by Simon & Schuster
in association with CLB Publishing, Godalming, Surrey
Title of the original German edition: Balkon-Träume
© 1994 BLV Verlagsgesellschaft mbH, München, Germany
© 1995 English-language translation CLB Publishing
All rights reserved
Printed and bound in Spain by Graficas Estella
ISBN 0-671-71426-0

# COLOURFUL CONTAINERS

SIMON & SCHUSTER

LONDON · SYDNEY · NEW YORK · TOKYO · SINGAPORE · TORONTO

# Contents

# *Introduction*

This book is aimed at people who would like to make the most of their containers. It shows how you can turn a grey area of the garden into a splendidly colourful flower-filled haven in which to relax on summer evenings. We hope that the designs we suggest will spur you on to create your own planting schemes.

It is amazing how you can conjure up different and very individual atmospheres by using simple materials and carefully selected plants. Anything is possible – a balcony with Mediterranean charm, a patio with the more rural character of a cottage garden, or a wildflower paradise.

You can create sunny places to sit amid greenery, back-to-nature children's play corners, green living-rooms in which to relax, and airy little gardens for the gardening enthusiast confined to an upper floor flat.

It is not just people with a garden who can live in close contact with nature – even a small balcony can offer a link with the colourful world of plants. Plants bring man into closer contact with nature, which helps to alleviate the stresses of modern life. Cheerful summery borders bloom in boxes. Every visit to the garden is an adventure, for subtle plays of colour can transform the smallest patio, or even the balcony into an oasis of blooms. With the variety of plants available, balconies can take on many new and distinctive

aspects. However, if your ideas are to succeed, you will have to choose plants that suit those conditions over which you have no control. A plant grown under optimal conditions will stay healthy and luxuriant and will bloom profusely. To help you find suitable container plants, this book is divided into sections on areas in full sun, in semi-shade and full shade. Within these categories, the plants are classified according to seasonal interest and colour. This makes it possible for the book also to be used to identify the flowers most commonly used in containers.

Many summer-flowering plants thrive both in full sun and in semi-shade. For this reason it is difficult to make a clear distinction in the portrait section, so some plants for the semi-shade also appear in the portrait section for containers in full sun. A table in the section on the semi-shade then lists the appropriate plants once again.

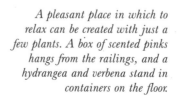

*A pleasant place in which to relax can be created with just a few plants. A box of scented pinks hangs from the railings, and a hydrangea and verbena stand in containers on the floor.*

In this book, you will be able to find the flowers best suited to the amount of light available. In the appendix you will find all you need to know about the planting, care and overwintering of your plants.

You are probably longing to get to work on your display, but there are two things you should do first: study the prevailing conditions carefully, and draw up a plan.

For example, on a south-facing balcony in full sun on the tenth floor of a block of flats, the climatic conditions in summer can resemble those in a desert, while on a north-facing, ground-floor area the conditions may be cool and humid. However, even for these extremes there is still a selection of plants that can turn such places into green bowers.

Areas with an east or west aspect have a more balanced micro-climate, giving you the largest selection of possible plants. If you have a west-facing space, you should bear in mind that rain tends to beat down heavily here and plants should be more weather-resistant. If you have an east-facing one, this will be less likely, but plants should be able to withstand the dry, cold east winds of winter. However, this only becomes an issue if hardy trees or shrubs have to spend the winter outdoors.

In our practical advice section you will discover what you can do

to help these permanent residents survive the winter.

Balconies 'in the clouds' may be buffeted by strong winds, and the choice of plants must take account of this.

Once you are aware of conditions that are beyond your control, you can then consider the amount of time and money you want to spend on your plants. Renewing the contents of containers each and every season takes some effort and can be expensive.

In the case of **successional bedding,** boxes and containers are replanted each season, while with **permanent planting,** hardy trees and shrubs and herbaceous perennials can remain in the same container for at least five years and require little care. A combination of both methods is also possible and is dealt with in the chapter on the all-season display.

An important consideration is watering during holiday periods, for containers can become a burden if you do not have a flower-loving neighbour who can look after your summer display. A sensible solution – and the best one for summer flowers – is of course automatic watering, but this has first to be installed.

In the case of balconies, should boxes be fixed on the inside or the outside of railings? Hanging the box outside the railings saves space, but the

excess water dripping down can be a nuisance if there are flats with balconies beneath yours.

Boxes on the outside produce the effect of a 'façade ornament' sometimes seen in holiday resorts. However, in cities, balconies are used more as living space and are intended to be enjoyed, so it is best to hang the

boxes on the inside. You can then watch closely as your little protégés grow and thrive – nothing escapes the observant eye of the gardener. It is also advisable to hang boxes on the inside of windy balconies at dizzy heights since this gives the plants better protection from the elements.

When planning your displays, do not forget to include trellises and supporting frameworks for climbing plants so that they can grow into vertical carpets of green. The resulting living walls will protect you from the wind and from nosy neighbours, and dull façades benefit from a green 'coat of paint'.

If you visit nurseries and garden centres, you will be overwhelmed by the enormous quantity and many different kinds of flowers and container plants on sale. This book will provide an invaluable guide to making the right choice. When you have settled on the appropriate groups of plants, you can then create your personal colour compositions, and your patio or balcony will become a delightful retreat.

Even the experienced gardener will find many interesting and new ideas for creative and varied designs in the following chapters.

*The bougainvillea and the marguerite create a holiday atmosphere all summer long.* Zinnia, Chrysanthemum, Pelargonium *and* Centradenia *are combined in the box to provide a colourful summer mixture. Regular and plentiful watering is vital to maintain this display.*

# There's always colour in the seasonal display

If you use annual spring and summer flowers, you will have the opportunity, in the perhaps limited space offered to create new combinations again and again. Since the life cycle of annuals finishes at the end of one growing season, it is not difficult to exchange plants that do not fit in well with your scheme for new ones. In this way you can design your display from scratch each season. As many summer flowers originated in hot countries, where there is only a brief rainy season, they are compelled to bloom luxuriantly in order to survive. This characteristic is an advantage for the container gardener. In contrast to a permanent planting scheme, a seasonal one can be designed afresh each year and even every season.

*A gardener's dream in a very small space. The dominant crimson of the busy Lizzies, petunias and verbenas is heightened by the strong bluish-violet of the summer-flowering phlox to provide a sophisticated colour combination. Variety is introduced very artistically into the design by the white sage and the attractive foliage of the bamboo.*

You will soon discover which plants are the most successful, and your favourite planting scheme will gradually emerge. Perhaps you like scented plants or perhaps you like growing fruit, vegetables and herbs – everyone has their own particular preferences. There will be plenty of scope for experimentation.

It has been said that a person who falls victim to a passion for gardening is never cured and finds himself becoming increasingly caught up in it. This is equally true of the container gardener!

# *Full sun*

A brief sunbathing session or a refreshing break under a parasol in the midst of a magnificent display of flowers – these are surely things anyone would enjoy. And you are in an excellent position to fulfil them if your area is in full sun.

*Like torch bearers of the spring, red tulips rise out of the deep blue sea of grape hyacinths and drive away the last vestiges of winter with their colourful display. Long-stemmed tulips are however prone to wind damage and should be planted in a sheltered place.*

**5 pots *Muscari armeniacum* (grape hyacinths), 3 pots *Tulipa* 'Couleur Cardinal', 3 pots *Tulipa* (Triumph tulips).**

## A lively start to the season

For a seasonal display, the year begins with the first rays of sun in early spring. The bees and butterflies are eager to take advantage of the first opportunities to find nectar and are attracted in large numbers by the splashes of colour. However, do make sure when buying plants that the blooms are still at the bud stage so that the pleasure lasts longer.

In contrast to the balcony or patio in semi-shade or full shade, temperatures in full sun can become quite high even at this time of year. It is not very unusual to be able to sunbathe in early spring, but unfortunately the flowers will be over more quickly if the weather is mild. Many spring flowers are borne on long-lived shrubs or trees. When they have finished flowering, do not throw container plants away, but plant the bulbs, trees or shrubs out in the garden.

Alternatively, you can remove the bulbs, complete with root ball, carefully from the container and put them in a box for storing in a cool place, ideally a cellar. There the bulbs can absorb all their moisture again and recover ready for next year. Only when the leaves are completely yellow should they be removed from the bulbs. Incidentally, bulbs are mostly sold in pots containing three to five bulbs in early spring, and you should plant them in these groups in a larger container.

There is something of everything in this box. Bright pink hyacinths tower over crocuses, snowdrops, Siberian squill and yellow whitlow grass, and are framed to right and left by primroses.

2 *Hyacinthus orientalis* (hyacinths), 2 pots *Crocus vernus* (crocus), 1 pot *Galanthus nivalis* (snowdrop), 2 *Scilla siberica* (Siberian squill), 2 *Primula vulgaris* (primroses), 1 *Draba aizoides* (yellow whitlow grass).

# Early spring: Taking pleasure in the first flowers

Even in early spring, in February or March, there is no need for your containers to be empty. They can be planted luxuriantly and very effectively with colourful harbingers of spring. In contrast to summer flowers, spring flowers can be planted very close together because the plants are fully grown and ready to bloom.

Early spring flowers are generally wildflower bulbs, and it is worth keeping them as it is fairly certain that they will bloom just as profusely again next year. However, to ensure that they do so, apply a light dressing of fertilizer both before and after the flowering period, and deadhead so that the plants' energies are not wasted in forming seeds.

For the sap to be reabsorbed from the stems and leaves, they need to be placed somewhere sheltered and shady after they have finished flowering. Do remember that there can still be frosts at this time of year. The bulbs were brought on in greenhouses and are consequently more sensitive to cold than those growing in the open. They should therefore be covered with newspaper or fibre fleece if frost is forecast. One small consolation: if the spring is not a sunny one, the blooms on these combinations of plants will last longer.

*For a simpler display, combine a quantity of snowdrops with winter aconites to form a white and yellow colour scheme. The highly recommended and sweetly scented tulip, 'Tulipa pulchella' has thrust up its leaves and in March it will unfold its purple star-shaped blooms.*

---

**3 pots *Eranthis hyemalis* (winter aconite), 4 pots *Galanthus* nivalis (snowdrop), 2 pots *Tulipa humilis* (tulip).**

---

# Prolific spring blooms

In April and May the days get longer and the sunlight increases in strength from day to day. In the containers only a few blooms still linger on among the harbingers of spring. If you go to a market or nursery during this time, you will find everything that spring has to offer. Now you can really go to town and transform your display into a sea of blooms. The boxes become spring beds in which the many varieties of tulip, daffodil and grape hyacinth compete to produce the most beautiful blooms.

In addition to flowering bulbs such as tulips and daffodils, particularly prolific biennials and, to an ever greater degree, long-lived trees and shrubs are on sale. How about giving like-minded gardening friends a surprise by presenting them with a colourfully planted spring container instead of a bunch of flowers!

*This box provides a delicate breath of spring with sweetly scented lily of the valley and sky-blue forget-me-nots.*

4 pots *Myosotis sylvatica* (forget-me-not), 4 pots *Convallaria mayalis* (lily of the valley).

If you have a very windy area, be careful to buy low-growing plants. Tulips with their long stems, for example, can easily snap in the wind. Ideal partners for tulips and daffodils are biennials such as forget-me-nots, wallflowers, pansies and daisies. They are especially suitable for underplanting and bloom well into May. They also help to make a smooth transition to summer bedding, which is planted out from mid-May onwards.

In contrast to the wild species, it is hardly worth keeping cultivars from one year to the next. Experience shows that their blooms are much reduced the second year.

Make a cheerful start to spring with this box! The individual plants are very cleverly arranged.

As the dominant plants, the deep pink hyacinths rise high above the others, attracting the first butterflies and bees with their scent. Loosely scattered among them are light-blue grape hyacinths and purple and white crocuses which form a pretty transition to the dense carpet of heather.

7 *Hyacinthus orientalis* 'Anna Marie' (hyacinths), 2 pots *Crocus vernus* (crocus), 2 pots *Muscari azureum* (grape hyacinths).

*Tulips and daffodils blend harmoniously among a green carpet of forget-me-not plants. The daffodils of the variety 'Tête à Tête' are not as large as the 'Sundance' tulips. A contrasting colour is provided by the Siberian squills which flower from early spring. The forget-me-nots will come into bloom slowly and will hold the fort until it is time for the summer bedding.*

4 pots *Tulipa greigii* **'Sundance'** (tulips), 3 pots *Narcissus* **'Tête à Tête'** (daffodils), 2 pots *Scilla siberica* (bluebells), 1 *Salix caprea* **'Pendula'** (pussy willow).

# *Introduction to the portrait section*

First a few words on how to use the portrait section. The plants have been arranged according to colour rather than by botanical name to enable newcomers to container gardening with little botanical knowledge to find their way around. If you come across a summer flower that you find particularly attractive, you only need to look under the appropriate colour to find its name. The specialist can also look up names in the index.

We purposely do not give too many recommendations as to varieties, since those on sale change from year to year. Also, plants are seldom identified with labels giving the exact variety name, except in specialist nurseries. We do not want you to go looking everywhere for a specific variety when the chances are that you will not find it. No nursery can hope to stock all the many varieties.

However, your local nursery or garden centre will probably sell a good selection of what is currently available.

The chapters are structured in such a way that you can start brightening up your balcony or patio at any time of the year. In the plant portraits you will find set out briefly and clearly the most important information on situation, compost, fertilizers, watering, propagation and anything else of note about the particular plant.

Only plants with similar requirements should be planted together since when you feed one, you feed them all. You will find details on their individual needs in the portrait section.

Now all that remains is to start transforming your chosen area into an imaginative and successful haven of green!

## *Galanthus nivalis*
(Snowdrop)

These ring in the spring with their bell-shaped flowers. They are at their peak very early in the year when frost and snow may still be on the ground. They are not effective seen from a distance, but their charm soon draws the eyes and heart of the container gardener. Even bees are attracted by snowdrops which provide their first drink of nectar of the year. Apart from the inner petals, which bear a green marking, snowdrops, as their name suggests, are snow-white.
**SITUATION:** sunny to semi-shade.
**COMPOST:** John Innes No. 1 or equivalent.
**CARE:** go easy with the fertilizer, otherwise you will stimulate too many leaves and will wait in vain for blooms.

*Snowdrops grow in profusion.*

*Daisies are generally available as double-flowered cultivars.*

**OVERWINTERING:** snowdrops are very happy to spend the summer out of doors and will become more luxuriant as the years go by.
**IN A BOX:** pages 14, 15.

## *Bellis perennis*
(Common daisy)

Nowadays the most commonly available, commercially grown daisies resemble their wild meadow counterparts only in the shape of their petals. The new cultivars, unlike the spring flowers from which little girls make daisy chains for their hair, mostly have double flowers and are available in white, pink and red. They are very compact in habit and bear many blooms. They go

particularly well with forget-me-nots and primroses. Even a box devoted entirely to different-coloured daisies has its own charms and is pretty to look at.
**SITUATION:** daisies thrive in full sun, but can also do well in semi-shade.
**COMPOST:** John Innes No. 2 or equivalent.
**CARE:** *Bellis* is actually a herbaceous perennial, but is grown as a biennial since it has a tendency to exhaust itself by blooming so profusely. The following year you will wait in vain for the carpet of daisies. Because the flowering period extends well into May, it makes an ideal transitional plant until the summer bedding can be planted out.
**OVERWINTERING:** it is advisable to plant *Bellis* out in boxes in March/April since autumn planting and overwintering are too risky.

## *Primula vulgaris*
(Primrose)

From December onwards, primroses are on sale in all colours as indoor plants. If they were planted out at this time, they would quickly fall victim to frost. Only in March/April can primroses be safely planted out on the balcony or patio together with daisies, daffodils, hyacinths and tulips. The primroses' vibrant colours make them easily visible from a distance. Apart from the bright basic colours such as white, blue, red and yellow, they also come in beautiful, delicate pastel shades that go very well

*Primroses come in many colours.*

with similar spring flowers. In addition to the compact, low-growing primrose types, there are also the cheerful, less compact polyanthus varieties that can grow 15-20 cm (6-8 inches) tall. Their ball-shaped flower heads sit on long stems which emerge from the rosette of leaves. These varieties also come in many beautiful colours from white to purple.

**SITUATION:** semi-shade and shade.
**COMPOST:** John Innes No. 2 or equivalent.
**CARE:** primroses and polyanthus like an evenly moist soil. However, their roots should not be allowed to stand in water, otherwise the leaves will quickly turn yellow. Horn shavings form the best fertilizer for mixing in with the compost.
**OVERWINTERING:** it is hardly worth keeping primroses in the display all year round.
**IN A BOX:** pages 14, 94-95.

## Narcissus
### (Daffodil, narcissus)

Daffodils belong to the same family as snowdrops but are later flowering, ringing in the late spring around Easter time. The big yellow daffodil is the best known of the genus which includes many diverse varieties. Many different cultivars are brought on early and are in bloom in March/April, and some varieties are even sold for indoor display in January/February. The large-flowered trumpet daffodils are not suitable for windy situations because their long stems snap easily. A much better bet are the cultivars derived from the low-growing, appealing *Narcissus cyclamineus*.

The most widely available variety is 'Tête à Tête' which has reflexed petals rather like a cyclamen. If you do decide on the big yellow trumpets, you will have to stake them.
**SITUATION:** sunny.
**COMPOST:** John Innes No. 2 or equivalent.
**PLANTING:** if you want to get ready for spring during the autumn, you can plant out bulbs in September or October at the latest.
**CARE:** you must watch out for late frosts in early spring, otherwise the daffodils will not make it through to Easter. Remove the dead heads immediately, or the plants will waste energy making seeds.
**IN A BOX:** pages 18, 24-25, 94-95, 110.

*Small 'Tête à Tête' daffodils and larger, paler 'Ice Follies'.*

*The daffodil variety 'Minnow' is no larger than the grape hyacinths.*

*The winter aconite blooms from February onwards.*

## Eranthis hyemalis

(Winter aconite)

If you look closely at the blooms, you will see that this plant is related to the *Ranunculus* genus. The winter aconite blooms even if there is snow on the ground in February, at the same time as the snowdrop. A circle of leaves surrounds the yellow blooms like a ruff. Winter aconites go well with white or purple anemones, snowdrops, Siberian squills and fritillaries.
**SITUATION:** semi-shade.
**COMPOST:** John Innes No. 1 or equivalent.
**CARE:** undemanding.
**OVERWINTERING:** in rough layers in a cool room.
**IN THE BOX:** page 15.

## Cheiranthus cheiri

(Wallflower)

The wallflower is an ancient cultivated plant that comes in brownish red and mauve as well as brilliant yellow. It blooms from April to June and imparts a very intense scent of violets. For container use there are special low-growing varieties. Dwarf wallflowers with double blooms grow no higher than 20 cm (8 inches). You will not have the heart to tear this sweet-scented guest out of the soil at the height of its flowering period – about mid-May. To get round this, you will need a second set of boxes to take the summer bedding. While the flowers planted for high summer grow to their full size, the wallflowers can continue to scent the air.

*Wallflowers have a similar scent to violets.*

*The 'Jolly Joker' pansy in orange and purple.*

A classic combination is wallflowers with forget-me-nots, tulips, daisies and pansies.
**SITUATION:** sunny to semi-shade.
**COMPOST:** John Innes No. 2 or equivalent, chalky compost (if necessary add loam and garden compost).
**CARE:** deadheads must be removed. Avoid waterlogging and do not let the root ball dry out.
**OVERWINTERING:** like pansies, wallflowers are biennials. Sometimes it is surprisingly difficult to find them in nurseries, even though they should be in every display. They are sown in May of the previous year and must spend the winter well covered.

## Viola wittrockiana hybrids
(Pansy)

Pansies are cheerful little flowers, very rewarding to grow and very modest in their requirements. The older varieties have a certain nostalgic appeal, the newer ones less so. Pansies offer an inexhaustible range of colour and some have quite large blooms. They can be roughly divided into two groups:

**1. Early-flowering varieties** bear a few flowers into the autumn of the year they are sown, but reach their peak the following spring. Many single-coloured varieties belong to this group.

**2. Late-flowering varieties** start their main flowering period in mid-May and produce blooms continuously until August. These varieties offer all kinds of interesting colours and colour combinations. The mini pansies and horned violets *(Viola cornuta)* are also very rewarding, flowering profusely throughout the year. If you want to start your pansy display in autumn, you will need the early-flowering varieties. Since pansies are very easy to grow, they are ideal for inexperienced container gardeners. Pansies look good alone or combined with tulips, daffodils and shrubs (see the all-season display, pages 154-155).

**SITUATION:** pansies grow best in semi-shade. If they are in full sun, you must not forget to water them.

**COMPOST:** John Innes No. 1 or equivalent.

**CARE:** undemanding. Remove dead blooms. They react badly to overfeeding. Keep the compost evenly moist.

**GROWING FROM SEED:** if you want to grow pansies from seed, you will need to sow in June.

*Double Persian buttercups are especially picturesque.*

## Ranunculus asiaticus
(Persian buttercup)

Like winter aconites, Persian buttercups belong to the Ranunculus genus. They are on sale from April onwards in white, yellow, orange and red. A box filled only with Persian buttercups looks very decorative, and many people like to fill a container just with different coloured blooms. With their rounded shape and double flowers they are reminiscent of peonies. They grow to 20-30 cm (8-12 inches) and go well with red tulips which also require frequent feeding.

**SITUATION:** sunny.

**COMPOST:** John Innes No. 3 or equivalent.

**CARE:** if you do not want to buy plants in full bloom, place tubers 15 cm (6 inches) apart in boxes in March. They are not totally hardy and require protection if frost is forecast.

**OVERWINTERING:** the tubers are taken out in autumn and overwintered in a cool place.

*Long-stemmed tulips should be placed in containers on the floor out of the wind.*

## *Tulipa*
(Tulip)

Tulips with their bright colours form the centrepiece of the spring display. The tulip season begins in March and lasts until well into June with the late varieties. Choose the early species and varieties so that you can free your boxes in good time for summer planting. The wild species of tulip are excellent with their wind-resistant short stems. Snow, cold and rain do not affect tulips, since this is the kind of weather they are used to in the high mountains of their native Central Asia. In contrast to their sisters, the cultivated varieties, these flowers with their resistance to wind and weather are not prone to disease. By combining different wild species of tulip you can achieve a continuous flowering period of up to eight weeks. The *Tulipa turkestanica* leads off in February.

Tulipa *'Plaisir'*, Narcissus *'Jack Snipe'* and *'Hawera'*, Scilla siberica, Jasminum nudiflorum.

The white blooms in early spring look like stars that have fallen from heaven while everything else is still dormant. When the forsythia comes into flower, the pleasantly scented and graceful *T. humilis* follows on, a true natural beauty. The water lily-like blooms of the *T. kaufmanniana* also open at this time. These enchanting flowers, which are also known as water lily tulips, can be enjoyed until mid-April. The colours range from creamy white to bright red. At the end of March the enormous blooms of *T. fosteriana* open. This grows somewhat higher than the other wild tulip species. *T. greigii* follows at the beginning of April and is particularly striking with its beautifully streaked leaves. *T. praestans* bears several orange-coloured blooms on one stem. The cultivar 'Unicum' is striking because of its white-striped leaves. More unassuming, but all the more endearing is *T. linifolia*, which now reveals its bright red blooms, and *T. urumiensis* with its brilliant golden yellow flowers. These are followed by *T. clusiana* with pointed blooms in carmine and white. Bringing up the rear is *T. tarda*, which blooms into sunny May and is therefore better suited to a permanent planting scheme.

Low-growing and early varieties such as 'Princess Irene' can also be found among the cultivars. Tulips with long stems also have their attractions, but are only suitable for corners or for areas that are sheltered from the wind. When planted in a bowl, they can be placed on the floor or near the wall of the house. A harmonious combination can be created by planting one variety of tulip with Siberian squills, light-blue glory-of-the-snow, crocuses and dwarf yellow daffodils. Long-stemmed tulips go well with low-growing varieties of forget-me-not, daisy and pansy.

**SITUATION:** sunny.

**COMPOST:** John Innes No. 2 or equivalent. Tulips like chalky soil.

**CARE:** tulips like evenly moist soil but will not tolerate waterlogging. If you do not want them to die, provide drainage as described on page 186 before planting. After flowering, the seed capsules should be removed immediately to prevent the plants' energies being wasted in forming seeds.

**OVERWINTERING:** recommended.

**IN A BOX:** pages 12, 18, 94, 160.

*Tulip 'Couleur Cardinal'.*

### *Crocus vernus*
(Crocus)

From among the many species and varieties of crocus, nurseries offer primarily the large Dutch crocus (*Crocus vernus*) as a forced species in spring in white, blue and purple. The yellow-flowered varieties are derived from the golden crocus *(C. flavus)*. Give this attractive spring guest a position in full sun since its blooms only open in sunshine. Only then do they reveal their bright orange pistils and anthers with which they entice the first bees on to your display. Plant two or three pots of sturdy spring crocus in a bowl or combine them with other spring flowers such as *Primula vulgaris* and *Scilla. C. tommasinianus* blooms a little

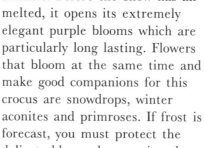

before *C. vernus* and is equally suitable. Before the snow has all melted, it opens its extremely elegant purple blooms which are particularly long lasting. Flowers that bloom at the same time and make good companions for this crocus are snowdrops, winter aconites and primroses. If frost is forecast, you must protect the delicate blooms by covering them with, for example, a large hat made of newspaper.

**SITUATION:** sunny.

**COMPOST:** John Innes No. 1 or equivalent.

**OVERWINTERING:** if you have been captivated by this pretty little harbinger of spring, you can keep the bulbs until the following year (see the practical advice section, page 187).

**IN A BOX:** pages 14, 17, 94.

### *Hyacinthus orientalis*
(Hyacinth)

The bewitching, heavy scent of hyacinths will be an experience you will never forget. From an almost inconspicuous wild flower, plant breeding has produced a vigorous plant that looks spectacular even from a distance. The range of varieties includes those with single or double flowers. Early-flowering and late-flowering varieties can also be found. Care should be taken when choosing the colours since many of these bright ones clash. Hyacinths are so striking in appearance that, when combined with other plants, only one colour should be represented if possible. It is then simple to select other plants to cluster beneath it and soften its rather formal character. Combine the early varieties with pastel-coloured primroses and daisies. Later varieties can be paired with forget-me-nots. Be careful when buying potted hyacinths not to choose any that are too advanced – they should open slowly. Go for varieties with simple blooms because the tall stems often fail to support the profusion of double blooms and soon snap.

**SITUATION:** give your guest from the hot countries of the Middle East and south-western Asia a warm, draught-free place, preferably near where you will sit. It will also do well in semi-shade.

**COMPOST:** John Innes No. 2 or equivalent.

*Bees find their first nectar of the year in crocuses.*

autumn. In mid-September the bulbs are planted out once more in the containers and must be well protected against the cold of winter.

**IN A BOX:** pages 14, 17, 94.

## *Anemone blanda*

(Anemone)

Anemones are among the most attractive harbingers of spring, with colours ranging from white through pink and light blue to lavender blue and deep purple. *Anemone blanda* likes rather more light than the native wood anemone, *A. nemorosa*, and opens its many-petalled, star-like flowers in March. It belongs to the early spring flowers, and so can be planted with crocuses and winter aconites. It tends to grow down over the container, softening the contours of the rather formal company of other spring flowers in a most appealing manner.

**SITUATION:** sun to semi-shade.
**COMPOST:** John Innes No. 1 or equivalent. Anemones love chalky soil.
**CARE:** keep moist and feed twice during the growing period, once before and once after flowering. Cultivation begins between summer and late autumn when the rhizomes are planted in damp soil and placed in cool semi-shade.
**OVERWINTERING:** it is possible to overwinter the plants outdoors in warmer areas, otherwise place them in a light, cool cellar.

*Scented hyacinths (above).*
*Anemones are easy to keep from year to year (right).*

**CARE:** remove dead flowers.
**OVERWINTERING:** it is worth keeping hyacinths for a second year, even though the plants will not have such dense blooms. After the leaves have turned yellow, the striking dark purple bulbs are taken out of the box and kept in a dry, cool place until

## *Myosotis sylvatica*

(Forget-me-not)

If you make a pilgrimage to the nursery in early spring to stock up with tempting spring flowers, you really ought to buy a few forget-me-not plants. Lay a green carpet of forget-me-nots at the feet of your tulips and daffodils, because when these start to fade at the beginning of May, countless little sky-blue flowers will develop on the long shoots of the forget-me-nots which will conceal the withered plants until well into May. The tulips that flower in May also look pretty when they rise like colourful torches out of a sea of blue forget-me-nots.

**SITUATION:** sunny to semi-shade.
**COMPOST:** John Innes No. 2 or equivalent.
**CARE:** they do not like dry soil and should be watered regularly. Forget-me-nots are biennials and must be sown the previous year.
**IN A BOX:** pages 16, 160-161.

## *Iris reticulata*

(Bulbous reticulata iris)

The early-flowering bulbous reticulata irises, on sale from March, are quite delightful. They come in many varieties in purple, light blue and pink. They stand proudly in the container and hold their elegant flowers high. In addition to looking distinctive, they also impart a wonderful scent of violets. They like sunshine, but will also do well in semi-shade. They look most effective when you plant several together in small groups. If you plant them in a box

*Forget-me-nots like damp conditions.*

*Delicate and frail, the bulbous reticulata iris.*

together with primroses, Siberian squills and snowdrops, the delicate nature of the smaller plants will form an effective accompaniment to the distinctive shape of the irises. Such partners also create the proper setting for the 'elegant' lady. The bulbous reticulata iris lives a long time and becomes more luxuriant from year to year, making it suitable for further cultivation. The optimal planting time is September/October.

**SITUATION:** sunny to semi-shade.
**COMPOST:** John Innes No. 1 or equivalent.
**CARE:** it does not like being waterlogged, so ensure good drainage.
**OVERWINTERING:** see practical advice section, page 187.

## Scilla siberica

(Siberian squill)

The Siberian squill is not as common a container plant as tulips and daffodils, but is popular nevertheless. In spring there are not many other blue flowers, but this colour is important if you want to create pretty combinations. Bluebells grow to a maximum of 20 cm (8 inches) and have small, star-shaped flowers. They are excellent as an accompaniment to wild tulip species and daffodils. By nature, they prefer light shade under trees and bushes. *Scilla mischtschenkoana* is a sweet little light-blue flower with an unpronounceable name that flowers in March. Somewhat larger flowers are borne by *S. siberica* 'Spring Beauty' which goes well with *Narcissus* 'February Gold'.

**SITUATION:** semi-shade.
**COMPOST:** John Innes No. 1 or equivalent.
**CARE:** keep bluebells slightly damp.
**OVERWINTERING:** well worth it.
**IN A BOX:** pages 14, 18, 24.

## Muscari armeniacum

(Grape hyacinth)

The magnificent blue grape hyacinths go well with daffodils and tulips, both as regards colour and season. Their inflorescences look like candles decorated with blue hundreds and thousands. Nowadays you can find light blue and white cultivars on sale as well as the typical dark blue varieties. You can

*You can buy forced Siberian squills in early spring.*

*Grape hyacinths come in light blue, dark blue and white varieties.*

buy them as forced young plants in nurseries as early as March. Grape hyacinths grow to about 20 cm (8 inches) high and are delicately scented. This undemanding plant loves sunshine but also does well in semi-shade.

**SITUATION:** sunny to semi-shade.
**COMPOST:** John Innes No. 1 or equivalent.
**CARE:** keep moderately damp.
**OVERWINTERING:** recommended.
**IN A BOX:** pages 12-13, 17.

# Summery oases

As mid-May approaches, container gardeners become increasingly busy. Once the danger of frost has passed, a new summer season can finally get under way. Markets, nurseries and garden centres are crowded with balcony, patio and garden enthusiasts. Now everyone wants to be sure of a green summer in their chosen area. The choice is bewildering and inexhaustible, and the range of flowers on offer grows with each passing year. Happy the man who knows what he wants! To help you with your choice, it is worth finding out beforehand what plants are in vogue for the coming summer.

*Many plants from the Mediterranean region are combined in this display. The strong pink of the oleander evokes holiday memories. The silk tree with its mimosa-like leaves will grow rapidly to provide shade. This deciduous tree can easily be overwintered in a dark garage. Even a little frost will not harm it. The sub-tropical atmosphere is reinforced by a terracotta pine cone.*

When will the flowering season reach its climax, when can you go on holiday, and how much work are you prepared to put in? You should answer all these questions before filling boxes, tubs, bowls and troughs with colourful blooms. Your local nursery may be able to plant your containers for you. Full sun offers you the chance to grow the widest range of species and varieties. The following suggestions for planting boxes are aimed at helping you to choose what will be most suitable. But first you should make sure that your display really does get enough sun. A south-facing area does not necessarily mean a full sun, since trees and houses in

front of it can mean it is in semi-shade. Only if the sun can shine in completely unimpeded, its rays beating down upon the boxes from the heat of midday until well into the evening, can you call it an area in full sun. In high summer it can quickly become too hot to sit outside in such a situation, so flexible shading is a good idea. The great advantage of full sun is that the popular oleander and other light-loving Mediterranean container plants will certainly come into flower without any problems.

*You do not always have to use flowers – even variegated mint can look beautiful. It also has a refreshing scent. Tickseed and Helichrysum ramosissimum crown this hanging display.*

1 *Coreopsis* **‘Sundancer’ (tickseed),**
3 *Mentha suaveolens* **‘Variegata’ (apple mint), 1** *Helichrysum ramosissimum* **‘Baby Gold’.**

*This area is so small that only one box has been used. To the right and left are heliotropes and in the middle a small-flowered variety of* Tagetes. *Below them trail geraniums that reach almost to the ground.*

2 *Heliotropium arborescens* **(heliotrope),**
1 *Tagetes tenuifolia* **(signet marigold),**
2 *Pelargonium peltatum* **hybrids (geranium).**

Summery cheerfulness is conveyed by this arrangement of the marguerite 'Schöne von Nizza' surrounded by lobelia. In the middle are the glowing colours of geraniums and verbenas, accompanied by the trailing shoots of the yellow creeping zinnia. Skilful positioning of the erect, semi-pendent and trailing plants has produced an interesting spatial relationship between the individual summer flowers. This box must be kept well watered and be fed regularly because all the plants require plenty of nutrients.

It is not without justification that the status of the sturdy trailing petunias as a container flower has been steadily growing. Here the large flowers of the vivid 'Shihi Purple' and 'White' complement each other perfectly. The white of the trailing petunias picks up the colour of the railings very cleverly. Both the petunias and the other plants require plenty of nutrients and are given the same treatment as regards watering and feeding. The one exception is the ornamental grass which, as a perennial with a low nutrient requirement, does not need much fertilizer.

2 *Chrysanthemum frutescens* 'Schöne von Nizza' (marguerite), 2 *Lobelia erinus* (lobelia), 2 *Pelargonium* zonal hybrids 'Tavira' (geranium), 4 *Verbena* hybrids 'Sparkle' (verbena), 2 *Sanvitalia procumbens* (creeping zinnia), 3 *Tagetes patula nana* 'Orange Hero' (French marigold).

6 *Petunia surfinia* 'Shihi Purple' and 'White' (Surfinia petunias), 1 *Bidens ferulifolia* 'Goldmarie' (golden goddess), 1 *Panicum virgatum* 'Strictum' (ornamental grass), 1 *Chrysanthemum frutescens* (marguerite), 1 *Diascia vigilis* 'Elliot's Variety'.

The floral flamboyance of this summer grouping is eye-catching from quite a distance away. The strong colours of the *Tagetes* and the dark purple heliotrope are intensified by their juxtaposition. However, a colourful spectacle like this, that is designed to be viewed from a distance, can be quite overpowering when seen close to.

3 *Pelargonium* zonal hybrids 'Mars' (geranium), 3 *Tagetes* 'Hero Gelb' (marigold), 2 *Heliotropium arborescens* 'Marine' (heliotrope), 4 *Lobelia erinus compacta* 'Blaue Perle' (lobelia).

This colourful summer grouping gives a likeable and playful impression. The sulphur yellow flowers of the African marigolds provide a focal point among the delicate filigree of the other plants. The geranium glows from among the extravagant mass of pink tobacco plant blooms. The underplanted lobelias form beautiful, compact cushions and the verbena flowers hang down from the box to make an edging. This combination requires plenty of watering and feeding, since this enables the plants to grow quickly to cover up dead blooms and produce new ones. Deadheading is therefore not necessary except in the case of the marigold blooms which would otherwise rot.

2 *Nicotiana x sanderae* **'Zartrosa Gnom'** (tobacco plant), 1 *Pelargonium* zonal hybrid **'Mars'** (geranium), 3 *Lobelia erinus compacta* **'Blue Moon'** (lobelia), 2 *Tagetes erecta* **'First Lady'** (African marigold), 2 *Verbena tenera* **'Kleopatra'** (verbena).

An absolutely rainproof combination. The bright bluish-purple of the *Scaevola aemula* is complemented very tastefully by the delicate pink of the *Diascia vigilis* and the trailing verbena. Both flower without a break all summer long. The long panicles of the *D. vigilis* are removed after the first main flowering. Otherwise this sturdy combination of plants is easy to look after. However, they do need plenty of water and plant food if they are to flower continuously.

1 *Diascia vigilis*, 1 *Scaevola aemula*, 1 *Mentha suaveolens* 'Variegata' (apple mint), 1 *Verbena tenera* 'Kleopatra' (verbena).

The flowers in this box form an exploding firework of colour and delight the viewer with their simple, summery cheerfulness. The double carnations in the middle form the focal point. The rose of heaven keeps on producing its light blue blooms all summer long. Sea lavender is popular in dried flower arrangements, being harvested at the height of its flowering period and hung upside down to dry. Be sparing when feeding this grouping – only the carnations require sufficient nutrients for flower formation. They should also be regularly deadheaded.

2 *Dianthus caryophyllus* (carnation), 2 *Silene coeli-rosa* 'Blauer Engel' (rose of heaven), 2 *Limonium sinuatum* (sea lavender).

This display portrays the romantic side of summer. The sun gleams gently through the petals of the deep pink verbenas as they rise up out of the box like little points of light. These are joined by the graduated pinkish-purple tones of the geraniums and lobelias of the underplanting. The white flowers of the ageratum sparkle very delicately beneath the roof of blooms. To the right and left, sweet alyssum adds a magic

4 *Verbena canadensis* 'Perfecta' (verbena), 2 *Pelargonium peltatum* hybrids 'Admiral Bouvet' (geranium), 2 *Lobelia erinus compacta* 'Rosamunde' (lobelia), 2 *Lobularia maritima* 'Snowdrift' (sweet alyssum), 2 *Ageratum houstonianum* 'Hawaii' (ageratum).

The flower heads of the geraniums glow merrily like red balls among this summer grouping. They create a very attractive flowing link between the white marguerites and the blue lobelias. The marguerites and lobelias must be vigorously cut back after the first main flowering period so that they can start producing a second round of blooms. The geraniums will be the main focus of interest during this time and will continue to bloom tirelessly provided they are given fertilizer frequently.

3 *Chrysanthemum frutescens* 'Vera' (marguerite), 4 *Lobelia erinus* 'Sapphire' (lobelia), 2 *Pelargonium peltatum* hybrids (geranium).

A wild, romantic planting with small-flowered plants and variegated decorative foliage. The two pink roses of heaven were grown from seed in the early spring and the lobelia is from the previous year. The sturdy white and green *Plectranthus forsteri* with its interesting, aromatic leaves is already almost taking up too much space. The feverfew and *Senecio* were only introduced into this box to fill the holes left by summer flowers that had already finished blooming. This group is very happy if fed with a moderate amount of fertilizer.

2 *Silene coeli-rosa* 'Rosa Engel' (rose of heaven), 1 *Senecio*, 1 *Chrysanthemum parthenium* 'Schneekrone' (feverfew), 1 *Lobelia erinus* 'Richardii' (Lobelia), 1 *Plectranthus coleoides* 'Variegata'.

There is no dominant plant in this mixture, each plant giving of its best in equal amounts. Like brightly coloured party crackers, the red blooms of the trailing carnation *Dianthus caryophyllus* glow above the variegated leaves of the apple mint. The carnations have a scent that resembles allspice, and the mint imparts its typical fragrance. The zinnia and straw-flower complement each other in a harmonious yellow-orange. You can cut plenty of strawflowers for drying and the plants will still continue to produce more blooms. The *Brachycome multifida* is not yet fulfilling its function in the display as it will be a little time before it is in full bloom. With regular and moderate amounts of fertilizer and regular watering, all the plants will perform at their best.

2 *Zinnia angustifolia* **'Classic'** (zinnia), 1 *Dianthus caryophyllus* (carnation), 2 *Brachycome multifida*, 2 *Mentha suaveolens* **'Variegata'** (apple mint), 2 *Helichrysum bracteatum* **'Golden Beauty'** (strawflower).

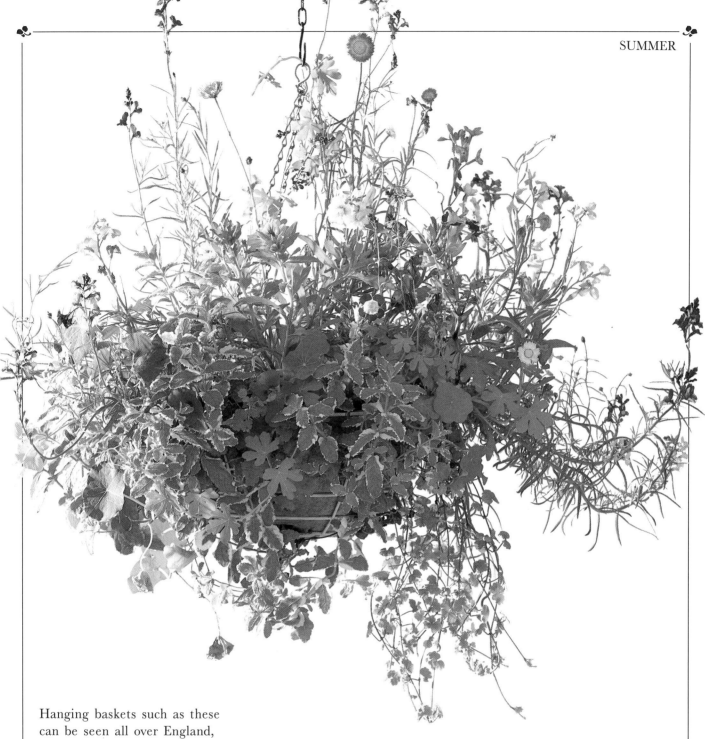

Hanging baskets such as these can be seen all over England, thriving without a great deal of attention. In warmer areas they do tend to dry out quickly and require frequent watering, but the plants like being high up in the air and grow better and more rapidly than identical kinds of plants down below in boxes. Simply line a wire basket with foam, fill it with compost and plant summer flowers both on top and through slits cut crosswise in the foam. The plants will quickly grow to form a dense mass which hides the wire. A magnificent show is however conditional upon regular watering.

1 *Mentha suaveolens* (apple mint), 1 *Mimulus* (monkey musk), 1 *Tropaeolum majus nanum* (nasturtium), 1 *Glechoma hederacea* 'Variegata' (ground ivy), 2 *Linaria maroccana* (toadflax).

Small but charming – this box is reminiscent of a meadow full of flowers with its simple but nonetheless atmospheric planting. Two 'Snow Lady' marguerites flank the golden yellow tickseed 'Early Sunrise' and are crowned by the scented, delicate blue larkspur 'Pacific'. The example shows that even a simple combination can be very effective.

2 *Chrysanthemum maximum* **'Snow Lady' (marguerite)**, 1 *Coreopsis* **'Early Sunrise' (tickseed)**, 1 *Delphinium consolida* **'Pacific' (larkspur)**.

The giant globes of the African marigold flowers exude charm and draw everyone's gaze. The *Brachycome multifida* with its filigree foliage and delicate star-shaped blooms creates a balance. The carnation blooms are not yet at their full splendour and, along with the *Asteriscus maritimus*, they must still assert themselves against the African marigolds. Moderate amounts of fertilizer do the daisies good, but also ensure that the African marigolds will not become too massive.

4 *Tagetes erecta* **'Perfection Orange' (African marigold)**, 2 Brachycome multifida, 2 Dianthus caryophyllus **'Balkonfeueur' (carnation)**, 1 Dianthus chinensis **'Feuersturm'**, 3 Dianthus chinensis **'Pluto' (Indian pink)**, 2 Asteriscus maritimus **'Gold Coin'**.

Requiring little care and attention, the two golden goddess plants are covered with hundreds of pretty flowers throughout the summer. As this plant grows at least 50 cm (20 inches) over the edge of the box, it can make a small area even narrower. The white blooms of the *Surfinia* petunia shine through the delicate foliage of the golden goddess and are flanked on either side by the blue *Scaevola aemula*. All three are equally vigorous in habit. The trailing carnation has chosen to grow in the other direction and gives pleasure to the neighbours.

**2** *Scaevola aemula* **'New Wonder'**,
**2** *Bidens ferulifolia* **'Goldmarie' (golden goddess)**, **3** *Petunia surfinia* **'White' (petunia)**, **2** *Dianthus caryophyllus* **(carnation)**.

This photograph shows an unusual but successful combination of *Scaevola aemula* and liquorice plant. The latter's pale yellow leaves go well with the mauvish-blue of the *Scaevola aemula*. Both partners have similar growth patterns and require regular, large amounts of fertilizer.

3 *Scaevola aemula* 'Blue Wonder',
2 *Helichrysum petiolare* 'Rondello' (liquorice plant).

This box is very trendy with its all-pink colour scheme. The tobacco plant rises above the smaller zinnias and verbenas. The elegant white of the container emphasizes the delicate pastel shades. Despite its soft and delicate appearance, this combination does not suffer when exposed to strong winds. The verbenas have to be regularly deadheaded otherwise they will set quantities of seed.

2 *Nicotiana sanderae* 'Rosa Gnom' (tobacco plant), 1 *Zinnia* hybrid 'Peter Pan' (zinnia), 1 *Verbena* hybrid (verbena).

This combination shines with the most beautiful colours that the palette of container flowers can offer. The sage towers above the sea of busy lizzies and phlox.

On hot sunny days it is vital that you do not forget to water this balcony box, otherwise the busy lizzies will become limp and will not survive the summer. The blooms of the treasure flowers and pinks struggle for a position amidst this luxuriant group.

4 *Impatiens walleriana* 'Accent Violett' (busy Lizzie), 2 *Gazania* hybrids 'Czardas Weiß' (treasure flower), 3 *Phlox drummondii* 'Blue Beauty' (phlox), 1 *Phlox drummondii*, Twinkle Series (phlox), 4 *Dianthus chinensis* 'Alice Zartrosa' (Indian pink), 1 *Salvia farinacea* 'Porcelaine' (mealy sage).

Here the summer sun is reflected in the brilliant yellow of the blooms. So as not to hide the view, no tall plants were used in this combination. The yellow creeping zinnias are framed by sweet alyssum, which crowns the box. The yellow slipperworts and the red verbenas must be deadheaded regularly to ensure continuous flowering. The yellow treasure flower keeps its blooms closed when the sky is overcast, opening them only when the sun shines.

Every spare space can be utilized if you are able to attach 'hanging gardens'. The flowerpot filled with *Nemesia fruticans* in pretty mauve hangs just above the box, providing a small area of shade. The *Nemesia* has the opportunity to develop fully on its own in the pot. The *Helichrysum ramosissimum* with its velvety blooms gives off a fruity scent, rather like pineapple. It flowers incessantly and does not need to be deadheaded.

4 *Verbena* hybrids 'Showtime Bell' (verbena), 2 *Calceolaria integrifolia* 'Goldari' (slipperwort), 2 *Lobularia maritima* 'Snow Crystals' (sweet alyssum), 2 *Sanvitalia procumbens* 'Goldteppich' (creeping zinnia), 2 *Gazania* hybrids 'Gartensonne' (treasure flower).

Hanging flowerpot: 3 *Nemesia fruticans* 'Woodcote', 2 *Helichrysum ramosissimum* 'Baby Gold'. Balcony box: 1 *Anagallis grandiflora* 'Blaulicht' (pimpernel), 3 *Nemesia fruticans*, 1 *Phlox drummondii* (phlox), 2 *Convolvulus tricolor* (convolvulus), 1 *Heliotropium arborescens* (heliotrope).

This combination is ideal for those who love scented plants. Stocks fill the area with their intoxicating scent. The convolvulus has twined itself round the box and complements the colour of the upright-growing stocks. Unfortunately, stocks do not produce a continuous display and have to be exchanged for another species after their main flowering period is over. China asters with their pastel shades would be ideal in this case to fill the gaps, and they would continue flowering well into the autumn.

4 *Matthiola incarna* (stock),
2 *Convolvulus sabatius* (convolvulus).

Boxes do not always have to hang on railings. If a living-room window overlooks the patio or balcony, this is a wonderful place for a window box filled with summer flowers which then peep in through the glass. The window box is planted with the traditional, tried and tested combination of geraniums and petunias. The petunias are the dominant plants in this case, and are discreetly crowned by two bluish-purple petunias. The petunias are still holding back, but during the course of the summer they will mix well with the geraniums. At their feet, the *Plectranthus forsteri* lets its long shoots trail far below the box.

3 *Pelargonium* zonal hybrids (geranium), 2 *Petunia* hybrids (petunia), 2 *Plectranthus forsteri*.

The slender, tall panicles of the violet and porcelain-coloured sage form a beautiful, shade-giving background for the busy Lizzies, which do not like too much sun. Under these conditions they will spread luxuriantly. The shoots of the verbenas hang far down over the edge of the box. The lobelias on the edge echo the strong violet of the sage and round off the whole effect harmoniously. The very sturdy, prolific and rewarding trailing verbenas set the tone for this planting. The splendid verbena 'bush' was achieved by getting the nurseryman to tie the shoots together so that they would grow upwards. This little bush will be cut back before spending the winter in the cellar, after which it will bloom again next year.

5 *Salvia farinacea* 'Porcelain' and 'Victoria Improved' (mealy sage), 2 *Impatiens walleriana* 'Accent Korallenrosa' (busy Lizzie), 2 *Verbena tenera* 'Kleopatra' (verbena), 2 *Lobelia erinus compacta* 'Blaue Perle' (lobelia), *Verbena tenera* 'Kleopatra', grown as a bush.

## *Chrysanthemum parthenium*
(Feverfew)

Sometimes you can find feverfew
plants in bloom at the nursery.
There are a few varieties of this
sturdy member of the family
*Compositae* that are of compact
habit and are therefore suitable
for a mixed box group. Feverfew
is a herbaceous perennial and has
little tufts of white or cream,
camomile-like flowers. The
cultivar 'Schneekrone' is
particularly interesting as it has
white tongue-shaped petals
encircling a cream, pompon-like
ball of tiny tubular flowers.
Typical of this plant is the
aromatic scent of camomile that
emanates from it when touched.
White, upright and easy-to-grow,
it is a valuable addition to a
mixed planting as it grows well
even in very exposed situations.
**SITUATION:** full sun, very weather-
resistant.
**COMPOST:** John Innes No. 2 or
equivalent.
**CARE:** requires regular watering
and fertilizer.
**PROPAGATION:** can be sown on the
windowsill from March onwards.
Sown outdoors from May onwards
in boxes, the plants will flower
very late.
**IN A BOX:** page 41.

*Feverfew has an aromatic camomile-like
scent.*

## *Callistephus chinensis*
(China aster)

The China aster is in fact not a
typical summer flower since it
only appears on the market from
late summer to autumn. It is not
worth growing your own since
they take a long time to develop
before they come into flower. They
are very prone to disease and are
therefore only on sale in nurseries
when they are in bud. They are
excellent as replacements for
plants that are past their peak
flowering period. For example, if
you have an ageratum that has
finished blooming, you could plant
a China aster in its place. The
pretty star-shaped flowers are
available in white, red or pink,
and it is not difficult to pick a
colour from this range that will go
with the combination already in the
box. The dwarf aster 'Pomponett'
is suitable for the balcony.

**SITUATION:** sunny.
**COMPOST:** John Innes No. 2 or
equivalent.
**CARE:** water regularly, but avoid
waterlogging and remove dead
flowers.
**PROPAGATION:** not worth it.
**IN A BOX:** pages 80, 83, 130.

## *Osteospermum eclonis* hybrids
Syn. *dimorphotheca*
(African daisy, Cape marigold)

This pretty, semi-woody perennial
has marguerite-like flowers in
white, pink or orange. The petals
are bluish on the underside. The
white varieties are very interesting
because of their spoon-shaped
petals which roll up to reveal their

*African daisies and dwarf marguerites in elegant gleaming white.*

*The China aster is ideal as a stopgap in late summer.*

## Chrysanthemum frutescens
(Marguerite)

The best-known container plant is the large-flowered marguerite that originates from the Canary Isles. A vigorous grower, it is often sold as a standard. In the normal box it grows too large and leaves its neighbours little space. However, we do not have to forgo its beautiful white now that the less vigorous cultivars 'Sugar Baby' and 'Whity' have been introduced. These go well in a group and flower all summer long. However, they do grow to 40-50 cm (16-20 inches) high and should therefore be used as the main plants in a display with other flowers. Apart from the white varieties, there is also the 'Schöne von Nizza' with its wonderful yellow blooms and 'Rosali' with pink blooms.

**SITUATION:** sunny to semi-shade.
**COMPOST:** John Innes No. 3 or equivalent.
**CARE:** it is somewhat time-consuming since constant deadheading is required to ensure plentiful flower formation.
**OVERWINTERING:** overwintering is only successful if you can keep the plants in a bright, cool place. During their resting period the plants should receive only very little water. The variety 'Silver Leaf' with feathery, bluish foliage is the easiest to overwinter, while the varieties with large, green leaves have proved difficult.
**PROPAGATION:** by cuttings.
**IN A BOX:** pages 2, 34, 40, 98, 103.

bluish undersides. In its native South Africa, Osteospermum blooms in the cool spring. For this reason it needs a long cool phase (vernalization) to ensure plentiful flower formation. You can be sure that the nursery has used the appropriate cooling method if the young plant already has buds. The cultivar 'Sparkler' has proved to be particularly free-flowering and is said to be the only variety to provide a continuous display. 'Sparkler' grows vigorously and needs a deep box. It is very resistant to wind and rain.

**SITUATION:** sunny to semi-shade.
**COMPOST:** John Innes No. 3 or equivalent, water regularly.
**PROPAGATION:** by cuttings.

*The undemanding* Sutera diffusus.

## Sutera diffusus 'snow flake' syn. *bacopa*

The pretty *Sutera diffusus* is affectionately called 'Snow White' in Switzerland. It bears masses of tiny white star-shaped blooms from the beginning of March until well into autumn. Its adaptability is phenomenal, thriving as it does both in sun and in full shade, although it only blooms sparingly when deprived of sun. It is an ideal companion plant since its discreet appearance enhances the effect of other flowers without drawing attention to itself. It does not require deadheading and always looks neat and tidy.
**SITUATION:** sun to semi-shade.
**COMPOST:** prefers John Innes No. 2 or equivalent. However, it will adapt to any type of compost.
**CARE:** requires regular watering. If the root ball dries out it will cease flowering and rapidly turns to 'hay'.

**PROPAGATION:** by cuttings.
**IN A BOX:** page 126.

## Lilium regale
(Regal lily)

The lily grows particularly well in containers since it needs to grow from shade into the light. The most popular is the regal lily (*Lilium regale*) with its large, white, strongly scented, trumpet-like blooms. The tiger lily (*L. tigrinum*) with its striped yellow blooms is also very popular among flower-lovers. If well cared for, the lily tirelessly continues to produce new flowers for several weeks.
**SITUATION:** the lily, which in nature primarily grows on the edge of woods, finds a container an ideal home. Sheltered, it can grow from shade into the sunlight as it would under natural conditions. It is a good idea to underplant with low-

growing herbaceous perennials or summer flowers, especially if the smaller plants come into bloom at the same time.
**COMPOST:** John Innes No. 2 or equivalent, porous and rich in humus. Good drainage is important so that the bulbs do not rot during persistent rain.
**CARE:** for the lilies to flower just as beautifully every year they have to be given regular, generous quantities of fertilizer. Applications should begin as soon as the leaves start to grow. Check when buying that the bulbs are not shrivelled and have intact roots. Do not buy the bulbs if they show any signs of mould, for they will not produce flowers. Pick red lily beetles off the leaves at regular intervals. If the beetles get a chance to lay their eggs, the larvae will eat the whole plant in a very short time.
**PROPAGATION:** not worth it.
**OVERWINTERING:** lilies are hardy in the garden, but in an unprotected container the bulbs can easily freeze. A dark garage or cellar is suitable as cool winter quarters.
**IN A BOX:** pages 30, 142, 165.

*Lily and heliotrope are an ideal scented duo.*

## Erigeron karvinskianus

This delicate plant, which looks very like *Brachycome multifida*, comes from Mexico. This type of plant does not require as much feeding and watering as plants with large, fleshy leaves, and hence is suitable for planting with similarly undemanding plants such as *Brachycome, Felicia* and *Zinnia*. The white, daisy-like flowers gleam delicate pink and grow to 1 cm ($^1$/2 inch) in diameter. They are produced in great numbers throughout the summer, making a thick covering that is marvellously suited as underplanting beneath container plants with a low nutrient requirement (such as *Yucca* and *Cordyline*). This daisy, with its dense, trailing habit, can also be used to great effect in hanging flowerpots.

Erigeron karvinskianus *does not like too much fertilizer.*

**SITUATION:** sunny.
**COMPOST:** John Innes No. 1 or equivalent.
**CARE:** water regularly and apply fertilizer sparingly.
**PROPAGATION:** by seed.
**OVERWINTERING:** you can overwinter *Erigeron karvinskianus* together with the chosen companion container plant, keeping both in the same pot.

## Lobularia maritima

(Sweet alyssum)

Sweet alyssum is, as its name suggests, a pleasantly scented plant suitable for container use. The flowers open to form puffy white clusters that have a honey-sweet scent from June onwards. In a box, sweet alyssum grows to produce long-lasting, overhanging cushions of scent. Being of spreading rather than upright habit, it is also suitable as a ground cover plant. In addition to the white varieties, there are also some with pink and violet blooms. When you buy the young plants they will look rather puny, but do not be led into planting them too close together in a pot. Sweet alyssum grows so vigorously that it literally explodes and closely positioned plants soon do not have enough space. If you plant them right in the front of the box, they will soon hang over the edge like cumulus clouds.

**SITUATION:** sun to semi-shade.
**COMPOST:** John Innes No. 2 or equivalent. The plants like chalky soil.
**CARE:** after the main flowering period, cut the plants back and they will come into bloom once more in late summer.
**PROPAGATION:** sow directly in the boxes from April.
**IN A BOX:** pages 40, 101, 104.

*Sweet alyssum's dense, overhanging growth.*

## *Bidens ferulifolia*

(Golden goddess)

Golden goddess bears countless star-shaped blooms in a veritable flowering frenzy from May until the frosts come. This summer flower with delicate, feathery foliage grows rapidly to form a loose, spreading plant. Before sending out trailing shoots up to 50 cm (20 inches) in length, it grows horizontally, which can cause problems in a narrow space. It is amazing how a plant with such delicate foliage can produce such a large number of flowers. They do not need to be deadheaded since golden goddess does not set seed, the faded blooms simply disappear under the new growth. As well as producing a profusion of flowers, the plant withstands rain very well. Even heavy showers cannot harm the flowers. Because of its prolific

*Golden goddess keeps on flowering.*

*All parts of the nasturtium are edible.*

growth it should be used sparingly, otherwise it will crowd out all the other plants. A maximum of three plants per metre (yard) is sufficient.
**SITUATION:** full sun.
**COMPOST:** John Innes No. 3 or equivalent.
**CARE:** because of its prolific growth, it requires large amounts of water and fertilizer.
**PROPAGATION:** by cuttings.
**IN A BOX:** page 45.

## *Tropaeolum majus*

(Nasturtium)

For the container there are the compact *Majus Nanum* varieties. Of striking appearance are the varieties 'Alaska' with its foliage mottled with white, and 'Whirlybird Scarlet' with its semi-double scarlet flowers. All parts of this plant can be used for culinary purposes. The tangy leaves can be used in salads and taste rather like water-

cress. The flowers are useful for decorating salads and cakes. Even the seeds, when harvested before they are ripe, can be preserved in vinegar and make a very good piquant substitute for capers. Nasturtiums look best when planted on their own in a box. There they can produce their gaudy orange-red blooms until well into autumn. However, the plants are susceptible to frost and must be covered if necessary.
**SITUATION:** sunny. Semi-shade is tolerated, but they do not flower as profusely.
**COMPOST:** John Innes No. 2 or equivalent.
**CARE:** do not allow them to be excessively moist and only apply a little fertilizer. If given too much, the plants will produce plenty of foliage but few flowers. During long spells of hot weather, they are

often attacked by blackfly. The quickest way to get rid of the insects is by spraying with a strong jet of water from a sprayer.
**PROPAGATION:** by sowing seed from April to May directly into the boxes. Sow 3-5 seeds at intervals of 20 cm (8 inches). After germination, thin out the seedlings to leave the strongest.
**IN A BOX:** page 43.

## Calceolaria integrifolia

(Slipperwort)

Nowadays you can obtain the beautifully compact F1 hybrids for container use which are very suitable for planting in mixed boxes. The cultivar 'Triumph de Nord' flowers very early and profusely. Calceolarias are among the more tricky container flowers to grow.

*Calceolaria is a somewhat difficult plant to grow.*

If they are kept wet, their roots rot and the plants quickly die. They also react to too much fertilizer and too high a pH in the growing medium by developing yellow leaves (chlorosis). You will often see calceolarias planted together with geraniums, although both have completely different requirements.
**SITUATION:** sunny to semi-shade.
**COMPOST:** because calceolarias are particularly sensitive to mineral salts as young plants, John Innes No. 2 potting compost is best.
**CARE:** deadhead regularly. Give small quantities of fertilizer regularly, otherwise the plant will stop flowering. A slow-release fertilizer is ideal.
**PROPAGATION:** the seed of the F1 hybrids requires lengthy preliminary cultivation and so is not recommended for sowing by the amateur. Propagation by cuttings can be carried out in autumn.
**IN A BOX:** pages 102, 179.

*The blooms of* Lotus maculatus *look like little tongues of fire.*

## Lotus maculatus

*Lotus maculatus* is an excellent plant for growing in a hanging flowerpot since it will grow trailing shoots two metres in length if well cared for. The orange and yellow flowers look like little tongues of fire, making the plant resemble a burning bush when in full bloom. The cultivar 'Gold Flash' is very free-flowering and resilient. It is easy to confuse this plant with the red-flowered *L. berthelotii,* which has somewhat more delicate foliage. *L. berthelotii* is more susceptible to disease and not so free-flowering, but otherwise has the same requirements as its yellow-flowered relative.
**SITUATION:** full sun. In semi-shade it only produces a few flowers, but just as much decorative foliage.
**COMPOST:** John Innes No. 3 or equivalent.
**CARE:** *Lotus* needs plenty of fertilizer and water. The compost should always be moist. If the root ball dries out, the plant will shed all its leaves.
**PROPAGATION:** by cuttings taken from the parent plant in autumn and set in small groups in the pot. Because of their large root growth it can be difficult to remove the young plants from the parent's pot. However, you must not damage the roots when potting on as the plants will fail to grow.
**OVERWINTERING:** they will survive the winter at 5°C (41° F), but should not be allowed to dry out completely. If they are kept too warm during the winter, they will not bear many flowers the following summer.

*Treasure flowers love strong sunlight.*

## *Gazania* hybrids

(Treasure flower)

Everything about the treasure flower indicates that it is a real sun worshipper. The large composite blooms in shades of yellow, orange and brown open in large numbers if conditions are suitably hot. Its foliage is frequently tinged with blue. A fair weather plant if ever there was one, it only opens its blooms in sunshine. The treasure flower is just what is required for the problem south-facing area for, as natives of South Africa, they feel very at home in strong sunlight. Varieties grown from cuttings and on sale in the spring are the best. They are more expensive than plants grown from a seed packet, but are more compact in habit, bloom more profusely and start flowering as early as mid-May. The bright yellow flowers and delicate, silvery foliage of the cultivar 'Sonnengold' and the lively, yellow-orange flowers with brownish-black markings of the cultivar 'New Magic' are particularly attractive. Only the dwarf varieties 'Ministar' and 'Garden Sun' are to be recommended from among those grown from seed. However, they only start to form flowers in June.

**SITUATION:** full sun.
**COMPOST:** John Innes No. 2 or equivalent, provide drainage.
**CARE:** the treasure flower always grows near water in its native country. This indicates that, although the plants love strong sunshine, they do not like drying out. During the hot summer months you should never forget to water them thoroughly. To ensure that they have enough strength to flower continuously, apply fertilizer regularly and remove dead heads promptly.
**PROPAGATION:** by seed in March on the windowsill.

## *Thynophylla tenuiloba*

*Thynophylla* is very like *Brachycome multifida* in both appearance and requirements. Of fairly spreading habit, the plant forms beautiful, overhanging cushions that are covered in small yellow flowers. Suitable companions for this plant are *Brachycome multifida*, African marigolds and zinnias. It also does well as ground cover at the feet of container plants, as a subject for a hanging flowerpot and in mixed boxes.

**SITUATION:** sunny to semi-shade.
**COMPOST:** John Innes No. 1 or equivalent, good drainage is vital.
**CARE:** this delicate plant only loses a little water through its fine leaves and therefore does not require large quantities of water. A low dose of liquid fertilizer applied once a week is sufficient. This plant flowers without a great deal of attention, is weather-resistant and does not require deadheading.
**PROPAGATION:** by seed in February at 16°C (60°F). It is only possible to take cuttings from the cultivar 'Sternschnuppe'.
**IN A BOX:** page 98.

## *Tagetes* hybrids

(African marigold, French Marigold)

The African marigold is ideal if you want a sturdy, striking container plant that flowers dependably over a long period. All *Tagetes* varieties grow bolt upright and form little bushes. The predominant colours are yellow, orange and brown, and these come in many gradations. *T. erecta* hybrids have striking outlines with huge, ball-shaped

Thynophylla tenuiloba.

flowers on tall stems. They are good for planting in containers but must be tied to a stake to prevent them snapping in the wind. New cultivars such as *T. erecta* 'Inca' only grow 30 cm (12 inches) high and can even be planted in boxes. The *T. patula* varieties, or French marigolds, are lower-growing still. The cultivar *T. patula* 'Yellow boy' tops the charts. Even easier to grow is the single-flowered *T. patula* 'Nana' because it is rain-resistant and does not require deadheading. The same applies to the delightful *T. tenuifolia,* which is quite different both in appearance and requirements from the other two species. It forms very decorative, compact bushes of delicate foliage. It flowers relatively late, from August onwards, producing extravagant quantities of single blooms. If you touch its leaves, they impart a pleasant, spicy scent of oranges. The clear yellow colours of these flowers can be combined with other bright blooms such as blue petunias or red geraniums. Because of its delicate foliage and looser shape, *T. tenuifolia* goes better with flowers of a wild type such as *Brachycome, Felicia* and *Zinnia.*

**SITUATION:** these plants, which are natives of Mexico, love hot sun, but they will also bloom well in semi-shade.

**COMPOST:** John Innes No. 2 or equivalent. Will not tolerate waterlogging.

**CARE:** the varieties with double blooms must be deadheaded regularly, otherwise they can easily rot in rainy weather. Use

slow-release fertilizer that does not contain too much nitrogen.

**PROPAGATION:** these plants can easily be grown from seed from March onwards on the windowsill and will bloom from June onwards. Be sure to use sterile compost when sowing. In mild regions you could also sow the seeds directly in boxes from the end of April.

**IN A BOX:** pages 33, 34, 36, 37, 44, 98, 99.

*Creeping zinnias and African marigolds bring summer sunshine to the balcony.*

## Sanvitalia procumbens
(Creeping zinnia)

An essential plant for patios and balcony boxes is the profusely flowering creeping zinnia, of prostrate habit. It harmoniously completes the whole effect of the summer container since it hangs far out and down over the edge.

The sunflower-like blooms, only 1 cm ($^1/_2$ inch) in diameter, are dotted throughout the foliage. These trailing blooms are excellent for use as underplanting in boxes. The cultivar 'Goldteppich' is of more compact habit and does not hang down as far. It has proved excellent in hanging flowerpots and also as underplanting for long-stemmed container plants. It flowers from June until well into the autumn and the first frosts.

**SITUATION:** sunny.

**COMPOST:** John Innes No. 2 or equivalent.

**CARE:** this plant requires free-draining compost. Because it grows rapidly, it needs feeding regularly. The root ball should not be allowed to dry out.

**PROPAGATION:** by seed sown in early March on the windowsill. If you do not want to grow from seed, you can buy the small plants cheaply at nurseries.

**IN A BOX:** pages 34, 92, 98.

## *Zinnias angustifolia*
(Zinnia)

The enchanting zinnia with its white, yellow or orange composite flowers is indispensable for container plantings that require little care such as Felicia, Brachycome, treasure flower, verbena, chrysanthemum and Thynophylla. You see the narrow-leaved zinnias all too infrequently in containers, although they are one of the most rewarding, upright-growing flowers. They form elegant, loose bushes about 25 cm (10 inches) in height.

*Zinnias are available in many colours.*

The cultivar 'Classic' with its single, orange-yellow blooms is very sturdy and resistant to rain. Also recommended is the cultivar 'White Star' which has creamy, very distinctive blooms.

**SITUATION:** full sun.

**COMPOST:** John Innes No. 2 or equivalent, but add some lime and sand to lower the mineral salt content. It is a good idea to provide drainage.

**CARE:** do not keep the compost too damp. You need to achieve a balance between drying-out periods and watering. For aesthetic reasons the dead flowers should be removed. To maintain a continuous show of blooms, give low doses of liquid feed at regular intervals.

**PROPAGATION:** by seed.

**IN A BOX:** pages 42, 102.

## *Punica granatum* 'Nana'
(Pomegranate)

In its native south-eastern Europe, the pomegranate is grown as a shrub, its foliage turning beautiful colours in autumn before leaving the plant bare for the winter. The dwarf form of pomegranate is ideal for growing in containers. Even as a young plant it has magnificent orange-red, bell-shaped flowers. It produces occasional small, round, leathery fruits, but these are inedible. With its profusion of blooms and ease of maintainance, the dwarf pomegranate counts as one of the most rewarding container plants.

**SITUATION:** a typical Mediterranean plant, the pomegranate loves a place in full sun.

**COMPOST:** John Innes No. 1 or equivalent. The pomegranate requires repotting only every 3-5 years.

**CARE:** this shrub has a low nutrient requirement. From August onwards, as with all trees and shrubs, no more fertilizer should be applied so as not to delay the new shoots becoming woody. Watering should also be reduced gradually.

**OVERWINTERING:** only when the thermometer drops below -5°C (23°F) should *Punica* be brought into its cold winter quarters. A dark place no warmer than 5°C (41°F) is suitable for this deciduous shrub, otherwise it will come into leaf too early. In spring, the pomegranate will be one of the first to return to its place on the patio or balcony, where it will slowly come into leaf again. However, if a sharp frost is forecast, you will have to bring the plant indoors again.

## *Cuphea ignea*

(Cigar flower)

The cigar flower is very popular even with confirmed non-smokers. The small, orange-coloured flowers with black markings do look very like glowing cigars. Its small leaves indicate that it does not need a lot of feeding and watering. Its spreading habit makes it ideal for planting in a hanging basket.

The unassuming cigar flower

*The cigar flower is of spreading habit.*

*The pomegranate is a deciduous shrub that spends the winter in the cellar.*

grows rather slowly and can easily be swamped by vigorous companions. If this happens, it will react by rapidly dwindling away. However, it will grow happily if planted with *Chrysanthemum paludosum* or *Brachycome* and will literally blossom.

**SITUATION:** sunny to semi-shade.

**COMPOST:** John Innes No. 2 or equivalent.

**CARE:** it will reward you if you can get the watering just right. If allowed to dry out for too long, it drops its leaves.

**PROPAGATION:** by cuttings.

**OVERWINTERING:** if you want to enjoy the cigar flower again next year, you must take cuttings in August, then overwinter the rooted cuttings in a cool place.

**IN A BOX:** page 179.

## Lantana camara hybrids

The small rosettes that go together to make up the blooms of these plants gradually change colour during the course of their flowering period, so that all gradations of colour can be found on the same bloom. The hybrids are available in many shades of white, yellow and orange through red to brown and violet. When grown as a standard it takes up the least space and so can be used in small spaces. If the standard is tall enough, the spreading crown of blooms will provide a shady spot. Do not forget to tie the stalk to a stick so that the wind cannot blow it over. *Lantana montevidensis* with its pinkish red flowers has a more creeping habit and is therefore very suitable for planting in a hanging basket. If you are lucky you will be able to find it in nurseries.

**SITUATION:** full sun.

**COMPOST:** John Innes No. 2 or equivalent. The young plants are very sensitive to too high a concentration of fertilizer.

**CARE:** *L. camara* hybrids produce many seeds, so all dead blooms should be regularly removed to ensure continuous flowering.

**PROPAGATION:** only from cuttings. It is not worth sowing the seed.

**OVERWINTERING:** this is only successful in a light place at a temperature of about 10-15°C (50-59°F).

## Nicotiana x sanderae

(Tobacco plant)

The tobacco plant is ideal for containers as it imparts a delicate scent in the evenings or after a shower of rain. It blooms reliably from June until late autumn with very little care and attention and grows to 40 cm (16 inches) in height. Its stems are soft and bend in even quite

*Tobacco plants are available in many colours.*

strong winds without breaking. Place only one or two dominant plants at the back of a box and arrange low-growing and trailing summer flowers in front. Tobacco plants are available in white, pink and red.

**SITUATION:** sunny.

**COMPOST:** John Innes No. 2 or equivalent, with lime and humus.

**CARE:** the tobacco plant blooms all summer long without much care and attention. The blooms are covered in sticky hairs and often stick to your fingers during deadheading. Cutting back after the main flowering period has finished encourages further blooms.

**PROPAGATION:** raising from seed is a job for the nurseryman.

**IN A BOX:** pages 32, 46, 100.

*The blooms of* Lantana camara *gradually change colour. Cultivar 'Lantana Prof. Raoux'.*

## *Antirrhinum majus*
(Snapdragon)

The flowers of the snapdragon are divided into an upper and lower lip. Only bumble bees are able to get at the sweet nectar that is concealed deep within the 'mouth'. If you want to look inside the 'dragon's jaws', do what the bumble bee does and press lightly on the lower part of the flower. The extra small varieties are suitable for container use and these are available in all colours and colour combinations.

**SITUATION:** sun to semi-shade.
**COMPOST:** John Innes No. 2 or equivalent, drainage must be provided without fail.

**CARE:** snapdragons tend to set many seeds which must be regularly removed. If you want the plant to grow into a bushy shape, pinch out the tips of the shoots.
**PROPAGATION:** from seed.
**IN A BOX:** pages 80, 99.

## *Dianthus chinensis* **hybrids**
(Indian pink)

This widespread and universally popular pink has delightful slit and fringed petals. It radiates endearing, nostalgic charm and has an aromatic scent. The flowers are frequently multicoloured, with speckled, flecked and star-shaped markings. A complete range of colours is available, so you should easily be able to find the one you want to complement your other flowers. These plants are broad rather than tall and are very versatile. Initially they grow upright, but then the stems hang over a little once they become laden with blooms. Of the many varieties, the compact and freely flowering 'Parfait' has proved particularly outstanding. From as early as the beginning of May, the blooms start to open one after another on the strong stems. The plant is at the height of its flowering period in June/July.
After that it has a rest for several weeks before developing new buds.

*Indian pink is available in every colour.*

**SITUATION:** sunny.
**COMPOST:** John Innes No. 2 or equivalent.
**CARE:** you will be rewarded with a second flowering period in the autumn if you cut the plant well back after the main flowering period. Indian pinks do not tolerate waterlogging and only require a small to moderate amount of feeding with a fertilizer containing a high proportion of phosphorus and potash. If you overfeed, the plants become 'fat' and you increase the risk of the base of their stems rotting.
**PROPAGATION:** by seed.
**IN A BOX:** pages 44, 47, 104.

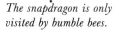

*The snapdragon is only visited by bumble bees.*

## *Pelargonium*

(Geranium)

The geranium is without doubt the star of the patio or balcony, combining as it does all the important characteristics that a good container plant should have. The blooms are very bright and are produced continuously in generous numbers from May until autumn without requiring much care and attention. In Germany, the splendid Bavarian farmhouses are famous for their 'geranium balconies' from which metre-long geraniums (several feet long), often many years old, hang in magnificent carpets of blooms. Each grower has his or her own tricks, often kept strictly secret, for

*The trailing geranium 'Mexikanerin'.*

ensuring these venerable plants continue to bloom at their best. Once, a farmer's wife told me her secret recipe for feeding the plants. She takes a handful of cow dung and dissolves it in a watering can full of water. She then adds a little of this mixture at a time to the can that she uses

to water the plants with, so that by the end of a week she has used up the batch. Unfortunately, this natural fertilizer is not available to people living in cities and, anyway, not everyone would fancy using it. Geraniums originally came from parts of South Africa where periods of drought are the norm. They grow there on the open veldt but can also be found in ravines where they only get sunlight for half the day. For this reason, geraniums are very tolerant of their situation and will also grow very well in semi-shade. However, north-facing situations in the cold shade of trees or buildings are not suitable. The more light and warmth the plants get, the more beautiful and luxuriant their flowers will be. The most commonly used geraniums are the trailing varieties or *Pelargonium peltatum* hybrids. You can recognize a trailing geranium by its typically shiny, five-lobed leaves and by its thin, low-lying shoots. Among the trailing or 'ivy-leaved' geraniums, the cascade varieties are the most worthy of recommendation. Their introduction revolutionized the container plant market, for no other plant can compare with them as regards vigour of both blooms and growth. At the same time, they do not need much looking after, since the single blooms curl up when they are over and are no longer noticeable. All the varieties with single blooms are weather-resistant. Trailing geraniums are not plants to be used alone and should be grouped with petunias and marguerites. Apart from the geraniums with

single blooms, there are also varieties with double blooms. Unfortunately these react very badly to rain. The blooms fail to open completely and begin to rot. They do best hung beneath a roof, where their magnificent colours will give much pleasure and they will be well protected from the rain. The cultivar that is least sensitive to rain is 'Tavira'. This plant has double red blooms and grows very vigorously. Apart from

the trailing geraniums, there are also the zonal geranium hybrids of upright habit. The trademark of this group is their round, downy leaves. Tried and tested cultivars are the vermilion-flowered 'Stadt Bern', and 'Rio', that has light pink blooms with a dark red centre. These varieties are easy to look after and weather-resistant. Each year, new varieties with ever larger blooms and more prolific growth come on to the market.

You can grow geraniums into a standard within a season without any problems. Scented geraniums are very distinctive – a few of the roughly 240 wild species of geranium stand out because of their scented leaves and beautifully formed flowers. They used to be popular as house plants and are at present undergoing a renaissance both in the house and on the patio or balcony. Essential oils are responsible for the scent,

*The double trailing geranium 'Amethyst' is beautifully compact.*

which is only apparent if the leaves are touched or rubbed. When buying the plants, you can choose the type of scent you prefer by rubbing the leaves. The flowers are of secondary importance in this straight-forward, scented plant, although they are very pretty if you take a closer look. In England, scented geraniums are sometimes placed in pots near the front door so that visitors are welcomed by a cloud of scent as they brush past them. *P. capitatum* smells of roses, *P. quercifolium* has a sharp, spicy scent, *P. crispum* smells strongly of lemon, *P. odoratissimum* smells of a combination of apples and lemon, and *P. citronella* conjures up a wonderful scent of lemon balm.

*An invitation to a summery breakfast amid scented, cascade and zonal geraniums.*

*The semi-double 'Lachskönigin' is one of the most popular trailing geraniums.*

*P. 'Clorinda'* smells intoxicatingly of eucalyptus, and *P. graveolens* is used in the perfume industry to produce geranium oil. We could go on and on describing the different scents, but suffice it to say that the collector will find plenty to interest him.

**SITUATION:** sun to semi-shade.

**COMPOST:** John Innes No. 3 or equivalent.

**CARE:** when watering, bear in mind that too much is more damaging than too little. Geraniums will tolerate a short period of drought, but they soon start to look unhappy if the compost is constantly wet. One outstanding characteristic of geraniums is their ability to tolerate chalky conditions – for this reason they even love tap water. Double-flowered trailing and bushy geraniums should be regularly deadheaded since faded blooms soon rot. If your geraniums are going to continue flowering into the autumn, they will need constant feeding to fuel their amazing capacity for producing blooms. Trailing geraniums and zonal geranium hybrids need a high concentration of fertilizer in **every** can of water that you give them (up to one

part per thousand). Scented geraniums require the same amount of feeding as plants with an average nutrient requirement. A special organic mineral feed for geraniums (Algoflash) is said to produce sensational results. This feed is added to the can at every watering. The nutrients are entirely used up by the plant, so mineral salts do not accumulate

*'Acapulco' is ideal for small balconies.*

in the compost. Using this method, geraniums 6 metres (20 feet) in length have been grown that have achieved an entry in the *Guinness Book of Records*.

If you want to overwinter your geraniums, you should cut the fertilizer ration by half from August onwards. The plants will gradually stop growing and will then be well prepared for a winter rest.

**PROPAGATION:** because it is such an important subject, propagation will be described in some detail here.

**1. PROPAGATION BY CUTTINGS:** the classic method of propagating geranium hybrids is by cuttings taken in August. These are then overwintered on a light windowsill in a cool room. Trailing geraniums in particular do not form many branches and should be pruned at the beginning of March. It would be a shame to throw away the new cuttings obtained in the process,

so plant these in a 10 cm (4 inch) pot of cuttings compost and cover with a perforated sheet of plastic. After a few weeks they should have rooted and can join the other geranium plants. Plant out in mid-May.

**2. BY SEED:** the F1 hybrids that can be propagated by seed are now increasingly to be found on sale. They are sown indoors in mid-December, for they take a long time to mature.

**OVERWINTERING:** you need a light but cool room if you are to overwinter geraniums successfully. The plants should be brought indoors before the first frosts, trimmed and preferably placed on a rack facing the light. The temperature should be between 5° and 10°C (41° and 50°C). Windowsills in unheated rooms

*All together in a box: zonal geranium hybrids 'Brasil', 'Rio', 'Bravo', 'Casanova', 'Alba' and 'Kardino'.*

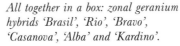

*Among the most decorative geraniums are 'Fire Cascade' and 'Ville de Paris'.*

are ideal, and best of all would be a greenhouse.

For geraniums the rule is, the warmer the room, the more light is required. However, the winter quarters should never be warmer than 10°C (50°C). While the plants are dormant between November and February, they should only be given a very little water.

**PRUNING GERANIUMS IN THEIR WINTER QUARTERS:** the tips of the young plants are pinched out in February and the old plants are cut back a little. They are then carefully placed in new compost without disturbing the root ball. From the beginning of March, watering needs to be increased and fertilizer given at fortnightly intervals. While the plants grown from cuttings are quick to put on new growth, the overwintered older plants take longer to start into growth and have to be forced in a greenhouse to bring them into flower sooner.

Geraniums kept in this way may win prizes in village competitions, but for most people it is all too much trouble and buying plants from a nursery is certainly a quicker and more convenient way to ensure a good show of blooms. **IN A BOX:** pages 2, 4, 33, 34, 36, 40, 50, 83, 99.

## *Diascia vigilis*

This nice, long-flowering plant has for many years graced the gardens of lovers of herbaceous perennials. More recently it has also been introduced into containers where it is often grown as a delicate hanging flowerpot specimen. The cultivar 'Elliott's variety' has pink flowers that open on the end of long panicles. It is upright and spreading in habit, is totally resistant to rain and looks in perfect shape even after a week of downpours. It flowers profusely from May until well into autumn. *Diascia* goes very well with plants with blue or white flowers that have similar requirements. Examples are *Felicia, Scaevola, Sutera* and *Chrysanthemum. Diascia* and *Scaevola* together make a very weather-resistant duo, complementing each others' colours beautifully.

Diascia vigilis *is extremely robust.*

**SITUATION:** sun to semi-shade.
**COMPOST:** John Innes No. 2 or equivalent. Good drainage is vital, since new shoots may die if the roots are waterlogged.
**CARE:** dead flower heads must be cut off following the first main flowering period.
**PROPAGATION:** by cuttings.
**OVERWINTERING:** *Diascia* is a hardy herbaceous plant, so it is worth trying to overwinter the plants outdoors. In very cold regions, the root ball must be protected from frost.
**IN A BOX:** page 38.

## *Nerium oleander*

Oleander

Everyone connects the oleander with the sunny Mediterranean area where it can be found on every street corner. It grows happily near the sea where it can always get enough moisture even in the hottest summer. Indeed, it requires temperatures resembling those of a southern climate if it is to come into bloom at all in more northerly areas. Varieties of oleander with double blooms have a pleasant, honey-sweet scent, but unfortunately they are not rain-resistant and often do not even come into flower. The varieties with single flowers are more rewarding. There is a dwarf oleander of less vigorous growth that does not burst the confines of the patio or balcony. The oleander needs to be in full sun, but the fact that it also requires plenty of fertilizer and water is frequently overlooked. Only when all its requirements are fulfilled

*Oleander needs to be in full sun*

will it develop into a splendid shrub. In summer, you should place its pot in a base filled with water for, contrary to most balcony plants, it likes having its feet wet. Oleanders can be obtained in many colours – white, pink, red, purple, and now also yellow.
**SITUATION:** full sun.
**COMPOST:** John Innes No. 3 or equivalent.
**CARE:** water copiously and apply fertilizer as you would for a plant with a high nutrient requirement. Oleander loves hard tap water.
**PROPAGATION:** in late summer, place cuttings in a half-filled glass of water until roots form. Change the water frequently. Once roots have formed, place the cuttings in compost.
**OVERWINTERING:** oleander will tolerate a few degrees of frost, but has to be brought indoors if the temperature drops below -5°C

*Verbena tenera 'Kleopatra' blooms all summer long.*

(23°F). A cool, light stairwell makes good winter quarters, but oleander can make do with a dark, cold cellar if necessary. Oleander has no place in an area used by children since all parts are extremely poisonous if eaten!

## *Verbena* hybrids

(Verbena)

Verbenas are among the early-flowering container plants and are very useful when creating designs for boxes because of their wide range of colours. Most varieties are upright in habit or slightly spreading and compact. Unfortunately, many varieties only have one main flowering period and are finished by late summer.

**SITUATION:** sunny.
**COMPOST:** John Innes No. 2 or equivalent.
**CARE:** because verbenas produce many seeds, the blooms must be cut off as they fade. However, it is often very difficult to differentiate between the buds and the dead flower heads. Liquid fertilizer should be added regularly to their water, which should be given a small amount at a time. As soon as the nights become a little colder and the leaves transpire less, the plants generally get mildew and do not look so attractive any more.
**PROPAGATION:** by cuttings and seed. *Verbena* varieties propagated by cuttings are more rewarding than verbena seedlings!
**IN A BOX:** pages 34, 40, 46, 73, 98.

## *Verbena tenera*

(Spreading verbena)

Two varieties that are particularly recommended for the container are 'Kleopatra' and 'Purpur Kleopatra'. These are more resistant to mildew and bloom reliably from May to September. Their deep mauvish-pink blooms go wonderfully with many other flowers. They grow vigorously and hang over the edge of the box, often reaching 1 metre (3 feet) in length. Spreading varieties of verbena work well in a hanging flower pot or even trained as a standard. They are good as ground cover for container plants and as underplanting in a box. They are weather-resistant and attract many butterflies. Other cultivars are 'Ophelia' in dark blue, 'Salome' in red and 'White Kleopatra' which, as its name suggests, has white flowers.
**SITUATION:** sunny.

**COMPOST:** John Innes No. 3 or equivalent.
**CARE:** this plant requires constant feeding and watering if it is to produce new flowering shoots continuously. It reacts very badly to drying out. Its flowers are sterile, so it does not produce seeds and does not have to be deadheaded.
**PROPAGATION:** 'Kleopatra' has to be propagated by cuttings and is therefore one of the rather more expensive balcony plants.
**OVERWINTERING:** since it does not lose its leaves, this plant has to be overwintered in a light place. If you want to overwinter valuable standards and spreading varieties in hanging flowerpots, it is best to take them to a nursery that is prepared to look after plants through the winter.
**IN A BOX:** pages 37, 38, 51, 101, 104.

*The large-flowered, deep crimson 'Shihi purple' is a superlative hanging basket plant.*

## *Petunia surfinia* hybrids
### (Petunia)

The *Petunia surfinia* hybrids come from Japan and produce an extravagant show of blooms. Cultivars that are commercially available are 'Shihi purple' and other white, mauvish-pink and bright purple varieties. They can produce metre-long (three-foot-long) shoots that are covered in brilliant blooms. If given the right amount of nutrients, they can grow at a rate of 3 cm (1$^1$/$_2$ inches) a day! They make splendid hanging flowerpot subjects, but are just as good in a colourful container grouping. White and deep pink pelargoniums go well with petunias since both types of plant have the same high nutrient requirement. Even white and purple varieties planted together yield an interesting combination

*The flowers of 'Blue Vein' are white with a dark blue centre.*

*The cultivar 'Pink mini' has smaller flowers but these are unbelievably prolific.*

full of colour and contrast. If you want to add *Scaevola, Bidens* and *Monopsis lutea,* you will be able to do so without any problems. These hybrids have such powers of regeneration that they can flower all summer long without having to be deadheaded.

**SITUATION:** full sun.

**COMPOST:** John Innes No. 3 or equivalent.

**CARE:** like geraniums, petunias need plenty of nutrients, otherwise

they do not require much care. If you are only able to give them hard tap water, the leaves may turn yellow during the height of summer because they cannot tolerate a large increase in the pH value of the compost. If this happens, use a soil acidifier plant flood that contains iron (see practical advice section, page 187). Within a short time the leaves will return to their bright green colour.

**PROPAGATION:** surfinias are propagated exclusively by cuttings.

**IN A BOX:** pages 10, 34, 45, 146.

*'Pink vein' has light pink flowers with a darker centre.*

## Centradenia 'cascade'

This plant first grows thin, overhanging shoots that are covered with pink flowers. In the course of the summer it puts out more and more strong, upright-growing square-stemmed shoots that are copper-coloured at first and contrast beautifully with the other green foliage. Flowers always start to form on the older shoots, so you should not cut the plant back. It goes well in a mixed planting scheme with other plants of averagely vigorous growth and is also suitable as a hanging flowerpot subject. Make sure when purchasing plants that they already have plenty of buds.
**SITUATION:** sun to semi-shade.
**COMPOST:** John Innes No. 2 or equivalent.

Brachycome multifida *also looks good in a hanging flowerpot.*

Centradenia *loves evenly moist compost.*

**CARE:** water regularly; otherwise this plant is easy to care for since deadheading is unnecessary.
**PROPAGATION:** by cuttings.
**OVERWINTERING:** cut back the plant and put it in a light, cool place.

## Brachycome multifida

When purchasing plants you should be aware that there are *Brachycome* varieties with different growth habits. For example, one important variety is the compact-growing 'Ultra'. It has sky-blue flowers and light green foliage, and is best suited to planting in boxes with other container plants. The variety 'Amethyst' has a looser, trailing shape and has dark crimson-purple blooms against dark green foliage. It is excellent in hanging baskets. It is happiest when planted with *Thynophylla tenuiloba* and *Erigeron karvinskianus,* but can also be grown alongside *Senecio* and treasure flowers without any problems.

**SITUATION:** sunny.

**COMPOST:** John Innes No. 1 or equivalent.

**CARE:** requires evenly moist compost and plenty of light. In semi-shade the plant becomes lazy and only produces a few flowers. It is easy to overwater, because the delicate leaves do not transpire as much as the large-leaved summer flowers. The needle-like leaves will then turn yellow.

**PROPAGATION:** by seed from March onwards at 20°C (68°F). Cultivars are propagated by cuttings and should be bought from nurseries.

**IN A BOX:** pages 33, 42, 44, 98, 146.

## *Ageratum houstonianum*

(Ageratum)

The compact-growing varieties are suitable for containers and are now available in several shades of blue and violet, and even white. The upright-growing cultivar 'Schnittwunder' is free-flowering and does not need much care.

**SITUATION:** sun to semi-shade.

**COMPOST:** John Innes No. 3 or equivalent.

**CARE:** requires humus-rich, well-moistened compost. Don't forget to water, and cut the plant back after the main flowering period.

**PROPAGATION:** with the introduction of F1 hybrids, it is now possible to sow the seeds on the windowsill in March.

**IN A BOX:** pages 40, 101.

## *Scaevola aemula*

This lavender-blue, semi-trailing plant with fan-shaped flowers fills container-owners with fresh enthusiasm every year. The fan-shaped flowers continue to appear in extravagant quantities without interruption until the first frosts. A native of Australia, this plant is available as a cultivar named 'Blue Wonder' that is absolutely weather-resistant and is excellent as a hanging basket subject. It is justifiably known as the best blue patio flower. It can be combined with the pink-flowering *Diascia* to produce a particularly attractive colour scheme. Its shoots start growing horizontally, then gradually hang down under their own weight. The compact cultivar 'Petite' is considerably smaller and does not grow such long shoots as its big sister. It is ideally suited to under-planting in a container with tall-stemmed plants or in window boxes.

**SITUATION:** sun to semi-shade.

**COMPOST:** John Innes No. 3 or equivalent.

**CARE:** you do not need to worry about the dead flowers, for they drop off of their own accord. However, the roots should not be waterlogged and hence drainage is vital. The plant should be given regular low doses of fertilizer and the compost should be kept well moistened. *S. aemula* is just as sensitive to pH as *Surfinia* petunias and their leaves may turn yellow at the height of summer, see *Petunia surfinia* page 71, section on care. Normally it is very resistant, but waterlogging for long periods weakens the plant and makes it susceptible to moulds.

**PROPAGATION:** cuttings root very easily in a glass of water.

**IN A BOX:** pages 38, 45, 46, 100, 103, 179.

*A real beauty of a display: the violet-blue* Scaevola aemula *and ageratum.*

Salvia farinacea *is a must.*

## Salvia farinacea
(Mealy Sage, Mealy Cup Salvia)

The pretty white or dark-blue flowering mealy sage is a must for the container. It can be combined with almost all profusely flowering plants and blooms from May until well into October. It grows upwards rather than outwards and attains a height of 50-60 cm (20-24 inches). The pale greyish-green, downy foliage forms a dense bush from which the panicles emerge erect like candles. The cultivar 'Unschuld' has white flowers and is a little monotonous in appearance. It should be combined with vibrantly coloured flowers. 'Viktoria' is not as subdued, for its flowers are an intense blue. The two together provide a nice contrast and complement each other marvellously. They have a pleasant, fruity scent.

Mealy sage does not know what bad weather is, for it is completely resistant to rain and withstands even the strongest winds.
**SITUATION:** sun to semi-shade.
**COMPOST:** John Innes No. 2 or equivalent.
**CARE:** mealy sage needs an average amount of fertilizer and should not be watered too copiously. With young plants, pinch out the main shoot in spring and they will then go on to produce 5-7 side shoots.
**PROPAGATION:** by seed.
**IN A BOX:** pages 10, 47, 51, 84, 101, 179.

## Felicia amelloides
(Blue marguerite)

The blue marguerite is one of the few blue-flowering plants that are of upright habit. It is a native of South Africa and so loves hot sunshine. Its magnificent blue flowers with yellow centres provide colour all summer long. Good plants to combine with it are *Zinnia, Gazania, Chrysanthemum paludosum,* red *Dianthus* and yellow *Tagetes tenuifolia.*
**SITUATION:** sunny.
**COMPOST:** John Innes No. 2 or equivalent.
**CARE:** it produces many seeds, but like the snapdragon they can easily be shaken off. You should not forget to water and give fertilizer regularly, otherwise it will stop flowering immediately.
**PROPAGATION:** by cuttings in spring taken from overwintered plants.
**OVERWINTERING:** blue marguerites are generally grown as annuals, but can be easily overwintered if a

light, cool (10°C or 50°F) room is available.

## Heliotropium arborescens
(Heliotrope)

This particularly valuable containers flower should not be omitted. Its vanilla-scented flowers not only delight the gardener but also attract hordes of bees and butterflies. In the evening especially, when the humidity rises, they impart their intoxicatingly sweet scent. They flower all summer long, provided they are fed and deadheaded regularly. The flowers are deep bluish-violet or light blue, and the plant can sometimes be obtained as a standard. Heliotropes can be easily combined with all the summer colours and complement any mixed planting outstandingly well. They are happiest with their

Felicia Amelloides *provides colour all summer long.*

*The vanilla-scented flowers of the* Heliotropium arborescens.

'heads' in full sun and their 'feet' in damp compost – that way they will bloom all summer long.
**SITUATION:** sun to semi-shade.
**COMPOST:** John Innes No. 2 or equivalent.
**CARE:** water regularly as heliotropes like evenly moist compost. Dead blooms must be cut off.
**PROPAGATION:** by seed or cuttings in August.
**OVERWINTERING:** in a light, cool place at 5-10°C (41-50°F) with a high humidity (greenhouse).
**IN A BOX:** pages 33, 36, 98, 99, 102, 103.

*Lobelia erinus* compacta *forms compact cushions of flowers.*

## Lobelia erinus
(Lobelia)

This 10-20 cm (4-8 inches) high African herbaceous perennial is grown as an annual in Europe. Originally, *Lobelia* had dark blue flowers with white eyes, but the cultivar 'Cambridge Blue' has grown immensely in popularity since its introduction half a century ago. 'Kaiser Wilhelm' has blue flowers and dark leaves, and there are also varieties in white, pink, and pale blue. The cultivar 'Compacta', as its name suggests, is of rather more upright and clump-forming habit. 'Sapphire' is a truly pendulous cultivar that can hang down to a depth of 40 cm (16 inches) and has a much looser shape. 'Richardsonii' makes an excellent hanging flowerpot plant, producing light blue flowers rather later in the summer. It does not manage to produce many flowers the first year, but can be

successfully overwintered.
**SITUATION:** lobelias do outstandingly well in semi-shade. In a south-facing situation you can plant them in the shade of other upright-growing flowers.
**COMPOST:** John Innes No. 2 or equivalent.
**CARE:** water regularly, but avoid waterlogging. In very wet years the plants may fail altogether. When young, the plants require plenty of nutrients and should be given small amounts of fertilizer frequently. However, they react badly to too high a concentration of mineral salts in the compost. After the main flowering period they must be cut back immediately, then they will give another lovely show in the autumn.
**PROPAGATION:** by seed on the windowsill in spring. The cultivar 'Richardsonii' is propagated by cuttings.
**OVERWINTERING:** only 'Richardsonii' can be overwintered in a light, cool place. The other varieties should be treated as annuals.
**IN A BOX:** pages 34, 36, 37, 40, 41, 51 ,82, 98, 101, 104, 116.

## Nemesia strumosa
(Nemesia)

Nemesia is a jolly little plant for people who like delicate container flowers. It is available in many pastel shades as well as strongly contrasting colours such as white, orange, pink and red. It is of upright habit, growing to 30-60 cm (12-24 inches) high. The upper part of the stems is covered in hairs. Nemesia is not really suitable as a companion for other plants.

Nemesia strumosa *is also available in two colours.*

On its own in a pot or filling up all the space in a balcony box, *N. fruticans,* with its snapdragon-like flowers on sturdy panicles, is more weather-resistant and very suitable for a mixed balcony planting. Two beautiful cultivars are available: 'Innocence' is white with yellow dots and 'Woodcote' has violet blooms.

**SITUATION:** it loves a sunny, sheltered place and gets very dishevelled if exposed to rain.

**COMPOST:** John Innes No. 1 or equivalent.

**CARE:** this nice scrophulariaceous plant likes to have its roots in well-drained compost and requires an average amount of fertilizer. After the main flowering period the plant must be cut back immediately to retain sufficient strength for a second flowering.

**PROPAGATION:** by seed in April at 13-15°C on the windowsill or from mid-May directly in the box. However, *N. strumosa* then takes longer to come into flower. *N. fruticans* is only propagated by cuttings.

**IN A BOX:** pages 48/49.

## Convolvulus sabatius

(Convolvulus)

This bindweed-like plant is also known by the name *Convolvulus mauritanicus.* It grows long trailing shoots on the ends of which pretty light blue trumpet-shaped flowers appear. The blooms open when the sun comes up and close as soon as the light fades. On cloudy days they have a rest and do not open at all! So it can happen that the plant is already asleep when you go out in the early evening. It does very well on its own in a hanging basket and grows more beautiful every year if overwintered under the correct conditions.

**SITUATION:** sunny, because the blooms do not open in semi-shade.

**COMPOST:** John Innes No. 3 or equivalent.

**CARE:** if kept well supplied with fertilizer, it will go on producing flowers into the autumn.

**PROPAGATION:** in autumn, cut off shoots 10 cm in length and push these cuttings into a mixture of peat and sand. Propagation by seed is also possible.

**OVERWINTERING:** after the flowering season is over, the plant is not composted, but spends the winter in a light, cool place. If the room is too warm, it will refuse to flower the following summer. It is advisable to cut back the shoots of older plants by two-thirds, since they tend to become bare at the base.

**IN A BOX:** page 50.

Convolvulus *sabatius needs full sun.*

## *Origanum vulgare* 'Aureum'
(Oregano)

You have not got the wrong chapter, for this is an ornamental variety of the familiar culinary herb and is intended to provide interesting variety in a container. Its bright greenish-yellow leaves are striking from a distance. Of compact and bushy habit, it is excellent as underplanting in combinations of yellows or as a complementary colour for red and blue summer flowers. Its make-up is identical to that of the regular herb.

**SITUATION:** sun to semi-shade.
**COMPOST:** John Innes No. 2 or equivalent.
**CARE:** undemanding.
**PROPAGATION:** by cuttings in August.

*The robust* Plectranthus forsteri *(right).*

*The yellow oregano is a sophisticated foliage plant (below).*

## *Plectranthus forsteri* 'Variegata'

*Plectranthus forsteri* is one of the easiest of all the container plants to grow. It forms long, trailing cascades of variegated leaves that give off a tangy, aromatic scent when touched. This Indian foliage plant is an excellent partner for red geraniums, the two plants intensifying each other's effect. The trailing stems can reach 2 metres (6 feet) in length.

**SITUATION:** sun to shade.
**COMPOST:** John Innes No. 3 or equivalent.
**CARE:** undemanding.
**PROPAGATION:** by cuttings in late summer.
**OVERWINTERING:** as for geraniums, in a light, cool place at 10°C (50°F). More successful with rooted cuttings.
**IN A BOX:** page 50.

## Helichrysum petiolare

*Helichrysum*, with its silvery green leaves, looks very pleasing and introduces variety into an austere plant grouping. Placed here and there among long-flowering plants, it forms an interesting link between them and gives optical depth to the scheme. If you put it with a group of plants that require only a small amount of nutrients, it will adapt to these conditions. However, if its companion plants are the sort requiring large amounts of nutrients, it can grow to a considerable size. The cultivar 'Silver' has fleshy leaves covered with silvery-white hairs and is of branching habit. If given plenty of fertilizer, it spreads over quite an area.

**SITUATION:** sun to semi-shade.
**COMPOST:** John Innes No. 2 or equivalent, needs good drainage.
**CARE:** undemanding - this is a robust plant.
**PROPAGATION:** by cuttings in August.
**OVERWINTERING:** Keep the rooted cuttings over winter.
**IN A BOX:** pages 2, 46.

*The silvery-grey Helichrysum petiolare.*

*The summer cypress.*

## Kochia scoparia

(Summer cypress, burning bush)

This distinctive foliage plant grows into a uniform, spherical bush with delicate, light green leaves. The cultivar 'Childsii' of spherical habit grows to a height of about 60 cm (24 inches) and stays green into autumn. The cultivar 'Trichophylla' turns red in autumn. The side nearest the house and thus afforded more protection stays green longer, giving rise to an interesting contrast in colour. Placed side-by-side in a box, the plants will make a small hedge that will give you some privacy. At the same time they make an ideal green background for colourful summer flowers.

**SITUATION:** sunny.
**COMPOST:** John Innes No. 2 or equivalent.
**CARE:** needs regular feeding since it grows very quickly.

## Mentha suaveolens 'Variegata'

(Apple mint)

Apple mint is very bushy and introduces an interesting texture into container groupings. It is very dominant in the way it grows and will quickly take over in a box, so must be used sparingly. It is easy to confuse it with *Plectranthus forsteri* 'Variegata', but instead of growing long tendrils it forms semi-pendent bushes. The leaves are light green with a creamy-white serrated edge and impart a typical minty smell when rubbed. It is also very good as a hanging basket plant.

**SITUATION:** sun to semi-shade.
**COMPOST:** John Innes No. 2 or equivalent.
**CARE:** undemanding. The more fertilizer it receives, the more it will grow.
**PROPAGATION:** very easy by tip cuttings.
**OVERWINTERING:** this is a hardy herbaceous perennial that needs a lined container to protect its roots from frost.
**IN A BOX:** pages 32, 38, 41, 42, 43.

*The bushy apple mint.*

# Plant combinations for the container in full sun

| Upright | Semi-pendent | Trailing |
|---|---|---|
| | **HIGH NUTRIENT REQUIREMENT** | |
| Chrysanthemum frutescens | Ageratum houstonianum | Bidens ferulifolia |
| Osteospermum ecklonis | | Convolvulus sabatius |
| Pelargonium zonale | | Lotus maculatus |
| | | Pelargonium peltatum |
| | | Petunia surfinia |
| | | Plectranthus forsteri |
| | | Scaevola aemula |
| | | Verbena tenera |
| | **MODERATE NUTRIENT REQUIREMENT** | |
| Antirrhinum majus | Calceolaria integrifolia | Centradenia |
| Callistephus chinensis | Convolvulus tricolor | Helichrysum petiolare |
| Chrysanthemum parthenium | Cuphea ignea | Lobelia erinus |
| Cosmos sulphureus | Dianthus chinensis | Lobularia maritima |
| Gazania hybrids | Diascia vigilis | Mentha suaveolens |
| Heliotropium arborescens | Felicia amelloides | Sanvitalia procumbens |
| Kochia scoparia | Origanum vulgare | Sutera diffusa |
| Lantana camara hybrids | Verbena hybrids | Tropaeolum majus |
| Lilium regale | | |
| Matthiola incana | | |
| Mirabilis jalapa | | |
| Nicotiana sanderae | | |
| Nigella damascena | | |
| Papaver rhoeas | | |
| Salvia farinacea | | |
| Tagetes hybrids | | |
| Zinnia angustifolia | | |
| | **LOW NUTRIENT REQUIREMENT** | |
| Agrostemma githago | Chrysanthemum multicaule | Brachycome multifida |
| Centaurea cyanus | Nemesia strumosa | Erigeron karvinskianus |
| Helipterum roseum | Thymophylla tenuiloba | Phlox drummondii |
| Nigella damascena | | |
| Reseda odorata | | |

## CONTAINER PLANTS CAN BE COMBINED AS FOLLOWS:

Applications of fertilizer should always be geared to the plants needing the least nutrients. If plants with a moderate nutrient requirement and those with a high one are combined, the amount of fertilizer given should meet the needs of the former, then all the plants will develop together harmoniously. If plants with a moderate nutrient requirement and those with a low one are combined, the amount of fertilizer given should meet the needs of those with a low nutrient requirement.

*Important:* plants with a low nutrient requirement and those with a high one should not be combined in the same box.

# An autumnal close to the season

Even if the magnificent summer display is drawing to a close, the container season is not nearly over. There may still be some lovely warm days, suffused with golden-red light from the autumn sun, already low in the sky. The Indian summer begins with its soft colours and envelops everything in special magic. Many of the plants that flowered in high summer now have to go, making room for the latecomers. Deadheads must be removed, and most annuals end up on the compost heap or in the compost bin. Winter-flowering heathers, asters, chrysanthemums, fleabane, veronicas and ornamental cabbage are already on display in garden centres, waiting for their big moment. Their deep colours will dress the patio or balcony for another few weeks in autumn finery.

The gusts of early autumn gales sweep over the containers and shake the flowers. The danger that long stems will snap is now at its greatest. Even before the first frosts, some summer plants will need to be got ready for winter. Fuchsias and container plants are placed in their winter quarters; dahlias and begonia tubers are taken out and prepared for winter. Do not forget to take cuttings from your favourite plants ready for next year. If you want to prepare for spring, you must now bring its harbingers out of the cellar, plant them in the boxes and insulate their roots well for the winter months.

At the beginning of November, when the first freezing cold nights have carried off the last flowers, only the ornamental cabbage and heathers still display their autumn colours. For all the others, it is now time for their winter sleep. There are still gardening jobs to do, like removing the remains of plants, emptying containers and putting garden furniture away for the winter.

If you want to brighten up the winter months, leave the compost in the boxes and make yourself a winter display (see page 90).

*On this autumnal balcony the flowers are still in full bloom. China asters, chyrsanthemums and sunflowers brighten up the last warm days.*

If you go to the garden centre in late summer, you will be amazed at how many colours and shapes the autumn still has to offer. Nature reserves a few absolutely beautiful species of plant that only reach their peak in the autumn. The first and most important group is of course the chrysanthemums, followed by the annual pot heathers and the perennial lings, and last but not least the wonderful grasses.

In late summer, when many summer flowers are past their best, you can get the nice China asters that are very useful as stopgaps. Autumn would not really be autumn without the abundance of sunflowers that are now on sale.

Autumn plants are bought while in bud and hardly grow any bigger on the patio or balcony. Repotting or planting in new compost is therefore unnecessary for these short-lived flowers. However, regular watering is important, for autumn sunshine and wind quickly dry out the compost in the boxes.

In October you can expect the first frosts. If you are careful every evening to cover the autumn beauties that are now in full bloom, so protecting them from frost damage, you will be able to enjoy an abundance of flowers until well into November. Deadheading will also extend the flowering period for a while.

*Here bright colours entice you outdoors in autumn. This combination is particularly successful because the compact-growing summer plants have a second flowering period in autumn, provided you have conscientiously deadheaded throughout the summer. The two summer cypresses rise up out of the box like two obelisks. Their rich green foliage is already tinged with decorative red. Even though the sun is no longer as strong, you must still water the plants regularly to ensure the compost is kept moist.*

2 *Dahlia variabilis* 'Mignon' (Mignon dahlia), 1 *Petunia* hybrid (petunia), 1 *Lobelia erinus compacta* (lobelia), 2 *Kochia scoparia* (summer cypress), 1 *Callistephus chinensis* (China aster).

The ivy-leaved geranium 'Fire Cascade' and the compact-growing geranium 'Tavira' are long-flowering plants and can remain outdoors until the first frosts. Earlier there had been a tobacco plant in the centre, but it finished flowering in August, it was exchanged without further ado for the China asters. These flowers, with their pastel shades, will last well into autumn if deadheaded regularly. Even at this time of the year, you should not forget to feed the geraniums. If you want to keep either variety for next year, it is high time to take cuttings.

3 *Pelargonium* 'Tavira' (geranium), 2 *Pelargonium* 'Fire Cascade' (geranium), 6 *Callistephus chinensis* (China aster).

*The dwarf double sunflowers 'Teddy Bear' here compete with the mealy sage in the evening sun. The Chinese fountain grass in the background brings a delicate touch to this rather formal grouping. This display, planted in late summer, will last for a long time if given plenty of water and fertilizer. The grass retains its decorative effect even in winter. It is frost-hardy and can be successfully overwintered if the root ball is protected.*

**4** *Helianthus annuus* **'Teddy Bear' (sunflower), 4** *Salvia farinacea* **'Victoria' (mealy sage), 1** *Pennisetum compressum* **(Chinese fountain grass).**

*If you return from holiday in late summer, you can decorate your patio or balcony again with these pretty plants. In a simple terracotta box, only foliage plants that reach their peak in autumn and provide interest well into winter were used. To the left and right are colourful ornamental cabbages in burgundy red and white with green.*

If you enjoy designing, how about arranging an autumn still-life like this? In doing so, you will attune yourself to the new season. Chrysanthemums are particularly suitable for such a design, and are available in many subdued shades of violet and red, but also in bright yellow. Autumn berries on flowering shrubs should also be included. Here the evergreen cotoneaster with its arching branches makes a wonderful framework for this composition. The ling in the shallow pot on the floor blooms for many months at a time. Grasses and grey-leaved plants complete the still life.

*Pennisetum compressum* (**Chinese fountain grass**), *Chrysanthemum x hortorum* (**chrysanthemum**), *Santolina chamaecyparissus* (**cotton lavender**), *Cotoneaster x watereri* **'Pendulus'** (**cotoneaster**), *Calluna vulgaris* (**ling**), *Dahlia* **hybrids** (**pompon dahlia**).

*The luxuriant* Calocephalus *weaves a fine mat of thin, silvery shoots that hang far down. The woolly, whitish-grey leaves of the* Senecio *tower above the box, its interesting, delicately sculpted leaves contrasting beautifully with the dark background.*

**3** *Brassica oleracea* (**ornamental cabbage**), **2** *Calocephalus brownii*, **1** *Senecio bicolor.*

### *Chrysanthemum indicum*
(Chrysanthemum)

Chrysanthemums are very popular once high summer has passed. They are ideal plants for seeing out the year and can easily be accommodated in containers and boxes. You buy them fully grown when they are in bud and place them in fresh, humus-rich compost.

The dwarf varieties are suitable for container use. There are compact varieties with small and large blooms. The small-flowered varieties that are grown as standards are also very popular and can be planted in containers standing on the ground. So you can have a little chrysanthemum garden during the Indian summer.
**SITUATION:** full sun, but since they are bought when fully developed they can in fact be placed anywhere.
**COMPOST:** John Innes No. 3 or equivalent.
**CARE:** Give plenty of water and fertilizer.

*The container star of autumn: the chrysanthemum.*

**OVERWINTERING:** this is possible, but not recommended because blooms will be sparse the following year.
**IN A BOX:** pages 85, 126.

### *Helianthus annuus*
(Sunflower)

The sunflower, which has inspired many poets to write romantic verses, is not really suitable for containers because of its enormous size. However, if you cannot resist this wonderful autumn plant, you can put it in a container in a place that is sheltered from the wind. The golden yellow daisy-like petals surround dozens and dozens of fertile tubular flowers, from which the well-known sunflower seeds will later develop. Radiating warmth and light from its golden blooms, the sunflower brings sunshine on to the patio. There are, however, many short-stemmed varieties that are more suitable for containers, and even branching varieties that bear a number of flower heads. A particularly good variety for the balcony is 'Teddy Bear' with double flowers.

There are even cultivars that do not have the typical sunny yellow flowers, but have reddish-brown petals instead.
**SITUATION:** sunny and protected from the wind.
**COMPOST:** John Innes No. 3 or equivalent.
**CARE:** To keep the enormous flower

*An autumn greeting: the sunflower.*

heads well-nourished, sunflowers need plenty of water and fertilizer. Tie dwarf sunflowers to a stake to prevent the stems from snapping.
**PROPAGATION:** Propagation is simple: the seeds are sown directly into the boxes from mid-April. Thin out the seedlings to leave the strongest. If late frosts are anticipated, you will have to cover the delicate young plants.
**IN A BOX:** pages 80, 84, 128.

### *Rudbeckia hirta*
(Coneflower)

The extremely beautiful coneflower is not a typical container plant, but should nonetheless not be forgotten. Some varieties grow to a height of 1 metre (3 feet), but those of compact habit are suitable for containers. The best such cultivar is 'Marmalade', which has bright golden yellow flowers and is of bushy habit. It grows to a height of about 50 cm (20 inches), has strong stems and is therefore also suitable for draughty situations. 'Rustic' offers a mixture of shades of yellow and red, and blooms from as early as July. A typical coneflower is 'Meine Freude' with its beautiful big composite flowers about 10 cm (4 inches) in diameter. It grows to a height of 60 cm (24 inches) and is best planted in a large pot and placed on the floor. It soon grows too big in a box. *Ageratum, Delphinium, Salvia farinacea* and *Lobelia* have proved to be good companion plants.

**SITUATION:** sunny.

**COMPOST:** John Innes No. 2 or equivalent, well-drained.

**CARE:** regular watering is important, otherwise the plant will soon wilt. Continuous deadheading is also required.

**PROPAGATION:** by seed in April. Transplant individually into pots and plant out after mid-May.

*The golden-yellow Rudbeckia 'Marmalade'.*

## *Dahlia* hybrids
### (Dahlia)

Everyone knows these very beautiful composite flowers. They are actually most at home in a cottage garden, but there are also dwarf varieties so that the container enthusiast does not have to be without them. These varieties, also known as dwarf Mignon dahlias, grow to a height of about 30 cm (12 inches) and are very happy in large containers. In spring they can be bought cheaply from nurseries as young plants raised from seed. The greenhouse plants are already in bloom then, so it is easy to pick out appropriate colours to go with other summer flowers. Dahlias come in a wide range of colours. These rapid-growing plants with cartwheel-like blooms reach the peak of their flowering period at the end of June. From the beginning of July they start to form seeds and this soon saps their strength. You should not be lazy about removing the seed heads, otherwise the plants will soon stop flowering.

The single-flowered dahlias attract bees, bumble bees and butterflies with their plentiful nectar. If you are a fan of the true, tall, cottage-garden dahlias with flower shapes such as the ball, cactus or pompon, you can simply plant these in a large pot.

**SITUATION:** sunny.

**COMPOST:** John Innes No. 3 or equivalent.

**CARE:** deadhead and water copiously.

*Pretty, delicate Mignon dahlias.*

**PROPAGATION:** by seed or division.

**OVERWINTERING:** after the first frost, cut the foliage back and put the pot with the tuber still in it in a cellar or other dark, cool place. Our grandmothers had to take the tubers out of the flowerbeds and clean off the soil that remained on them, otherwise they would have gone mouldy in the damp cellar. However, modern cellars are so dry that all the moisture would be drawn out of the tubers, drying them out completely. The tubers would not then have enough sap in them to put out shoots the following spring. Dahlias need time in which to 'tank up' again, so they flower late.

After mid-May the following year, the tubers and their pots are brought out of storage place and returned to their summer position.

**IN A BOX:** pages 82, 85, 114.

## *Erica gracilis*
### (Heather)

When the summer flowers have been cleared away and all is ready for the winter, this is the season for heathers. In early November, when it is already cold outside, the beautiful red of *Erica gracilis* brings colour once more and is a cheering sight. Combine it with chrysanthemums to make a beautiful, free-flowering duo. With the first severe frost the plant does suffer frost damage, but its blooms retain their colour until Christmas. Later, hoarfrost can still coat the dead flowers and bring a touch of winter magic.

**SITUATION:** sun to shade, since the plant is bought when already in bloom.

**COMPOST:** potting compost.

**CARE:** Before planting, dry root balls should be soaked in a container of water.

**IN A BOX:** page 17.

## *Brassica oleracea*
### (Ornamental cabbage)

You may have noticed colourful cabbages on market stalls in autumn. These beautiful cabbages are not destined for the cooking pot, but for the container, where their splendid colours strike an autumnal note. They are available with smooth, wavy or crinkled leaves.

*The magical colour of* Erica gracilis.

*The ornamental cabbage looks decorative for many weeks (below right).*

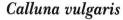

*An evergreen* Hebe andersonii *hybrid.*

Some are reminiscent of savoy cabbages, others of white cabbages. Inconspicuous at first, the cabbages change colour increasingly as the temperature drops, displaying shades of white, cream, mauve and pink. Since they tolerate light frosts down to -10°C (14°F), they retain their colours until well on into the winter. Only in early spring, when temperatures rise again, do the leaves wilt and the cabbages have to make way for spring bulbs and flowers.
**SITUATION:** anywhere, because it is already fully grown when purchased.
**COMPOST:** humus-rich.
**CARE:** give plenty of water and fertilizer.
**IN A BOX:** pages 84, 126.

## Hebe andersonii hybrids

*Hebe andersonii* hybrids make valuable evergreen container plants that are worth overwintering. These compact-growing shrubs grow to a height of 1 metre (3 feet) in their native New Zealand. Nevertheless, they are sold as autumn planting for the seasonal container. In August the racemes form in the leaf axils. They come in many varieties and may have white, red, purple or blue flowers. It is rather expensive to fill a whole window box with them, but the effect is most attractive. They go particularly well at this time of year with silvery *Senecio* and heathers.
**SITUATION:** sunny and sheltered.
**COMPOST:** John Innes No. 1 or equivalent.
**PROPAGATION:** by tip cuttings in summer.
**OVERWINTERING:** from the first frosts in a light, cool room (5 – 10°C or 41 to 50°F).
**IN A BOX:** pages 106, 126.

## Calluna vulgaris

(Ling, Scotch heather)

Ling, which is available from garden centres everywhere in late summer, blooms well into winter if properly cared for. It loves acid soil and, as a perennial woody plant, can be overwintered. The purple blooms go well with the strong colours of chrysanthemums.
**SITUATION:** sun to semi-shade.
**COMPOST:** ericaceous compost or other compost that has a low pH, i.e. is acid, and low in lime (peat-based compost).
**CARE:** water sufficiently, preferably with soft water. Do not allow to dry out in winter.
**PROPAGATION:** by cuttings.
**OVERWINTERING:** can also be overwintered in its pot. Cut the plant back in early spring to promote bushy growth.
**IN A BOX:** pages 85, 126.

*Ling becomes increasingly luxuriant with time.*

# Winter can be so attractive

Everything has been tidied up, the chairs and tables have been stowed away and the patio or balcony season is finally over for this year.

However, if you do not want to look out upon a bare area during the dark and dreary months of winter, take action now so you will not lack something attractive to look at. Unfortunately there are now no living plants suitable for growing on the seasonal patio, but you can still decorate your containers. You may find branches of yew, thuja, spruce, holly and box on sale in florists and garden centres. There is also a large selection of dried seed heads that look very pretty arranged in among the branches.

You can also decorate your boxes with twigs hung with berries, as provided by nature. Holly, rowan and cotoneaster berries, rosehips and sloes provide a colourful winter feast for your eyes and a vital source of food for birds. When all the berries have been eaten, you can fall back on the evergreen conifer branches. If you want to give yourself this pleasure, do not empty the boxes and containers in autumn, but simply cut down the greenery. The compost with its dense network of roots provides an excellent anchor for twigs and branches, and the moisture contained in it will keep them fresh for a long time. If you want a more colourful display, you can resort to the many weather-resistant lacquered ribbons, chains and bands.

Even frost-resistant earthenware figures and baubles look very attractive amongst all the winter greenery and liven up the containers.

Often just one box with winter decorations is enough to make things look less dreary. When Christmas time comes you can brighten up this display with fairy lights. You will not have to do any more work until early spring, for neither watering nor feeding are necessary. Relax and remember a year of successful blooms, and enjoy this quiet period with a cup of tea and perhaps a bulb catalogue!

*Thuja, yew and holly branches have been stuck into the box to form a small hedge. It serves as a beautiful green framework for the attractively placed seed heads. Thistles, persimmon and bulrushes look as if they have been coated with icing sugar and create a wintery mood.*

# Containers in semi-shade

A patio or balcony in semi-shade is of course the most usual situation. Usually a balcony faces either east or west.

The sun rises in the east, so mornings on the east-facing setting are the brightest time. With a west-facing situation, the sun comes round towards afternoon, by which time it is considerably stronger. West-facing areas therefore warm up much more and are consequently not suitable for fuchsias, begonias and busy lizzies. But the surroundings can also turn a south-facing setting into one in semi-shade – for instance, when a tall tree partly shades the area.

On the inside of balcony railings there is always semi-shade, even on a south-facing balcony, if there is another balcony overhead casting a shadow on it. You will also need to consider that a building casts a cold shadow, whereas the sun shining through the leaves of a tree creates warm, light shadow. Protected from the blazing midday sun, the patio or balcony in semi-shade provides pleasant conditions for people and plants without having to spend a fortune on measures to keep off the sun.

*There are unlimited opportunities on the setting in semi-shade. Here you can grow busy lizzies, fuchsias, abutilons and hydrangeas, and enjoy a view filled with greenery.*

# Colourful spring flowers

In semi-shade, spring also has a cheerful beginning. Nothing is missing, for almost all the spring flowers feel at home here. The container season can now get under way. Most of the spring flowers that we described for full sun do just as well in semi-shade. So the best thing for you to do would be to look at the portrait section in full sun and choose your favourite flowers in peace and quiet. There need be no limit to your gardening ambitions.

*This friendly spring group brings bright colours, makes you feel optimistic and allows you to anticipate the pleasures of the summer season. Pots of flowering hyacinths, daffodils, crocuses, primroses and Siberian squills (white variety) have been bought and added in mid-March to the dwarf willow that is a permanent feature.*

Narcissus *'Jack Snipe'* and Tulipa *'Mr v.d. Hoeff'*.

# A magnificent riot of colour

You can think yourself lucky if your patio or balcony is in semi-shade. Apart from a few exceptions, a container gardener can have everything he or she wants. Most summer flowers are just as happy in semi-shade as in full sun. Some summer flowers, such as *Osteospermum, Heliotropium* and *Pelargonium,* are sun-lovers, but they also tolerate semi-shade well. They do not produce quite as many flowers and grow more leaves instead. This can be an advantage for many plant combinations.

*On this balcony you are invited to tea in atmospheric surroundings. It will be very pleasant sitting amongst all this greenery. Begonias will tolerate shade, but they do much better in semi-shade. The trailing geranium does not flower quite as readily in the more limited lighting conditions, but still offers a pretty picture. The* Plectranthus forsteri *lets its colourful shoots trail downwards to provide some privacy. The grass* Miscanthus sinensis *'Silver Feather' hangs its leaves elegantly over the side of the box. Its special feature is its flower spikes, which appear in August.*

This box has not developed as was originally planned. The heliotropes were to have been the dominant plants and the busy Lizzies and lobelias were to have hung over the edge of the box. Instead, due to lack of space, the busy Lizzies have grown upwards. The plants make a colourful mass, and their random appearance adds to their appeal. Only the lobelias are still growing in their clumps, but they are gradually being hemmed in on all sides.

4 *Impatiens walleriana* 'Ballerina Scharlach-Weiß' (busy Lizzie), 2 *Heliotropium arborescens* 'Marine' (heliotrope), 2 *Verbena* hybrids 'Showtime Bell' (verbena), 4 *Lobelia erinus compacta* 'Blaue Perle' (lobelia), 2 *Tagetes patula nana* 'Yellow Jacket' (French marigold).

The yellow, compact-growing marguerites bring light into the semi-shade with their bright blooms. Here complementary colours are set against each other. The yellow of the marguerites and the dark bluish-violet of the heliotrope enhance each other. The *Brachycome multifida* in pale blue and *Thynophylla tenuiloba* in yellow moderate this effect somewhat. They have done well despite the relatively large amounts of fertilizer needed for the marguerites and the heliotrope. When they have finished flowering, the holes will be filled by other luxuriant plants.

3 *Chrysanthemum frutescens* 'Butterfly' (marguerite), 2 *Heliotropium arborescens* 'Mini Marine' (heliotrope), 3 *Brachycome multifida* 'Ultra', 2 *Sanvitalia procumbens* 'Sprite Yellow' (creeping zinnia), 2 *Thynophylla tenuiloba*.

In this informal group, the *Tagetes tenuifolia* clearly takes the lead and all the other plants have to assume a subordinate role. The yellow, small-flowered *Tagetes* is flanked by the scented heliotropes whose dark purple creates a clear contrast to the bright yellow, thereby enhancing its brilliance. The geranium trails elegantly over the edge of the box, but is very much a subordinate plant in this combination. It does not flower as luxuriantly as you would expect, but it nevertheless forms a pretty curtain of flowers. Even the marguerites have fewer flowers and the red and white snapdragons poke their heads cautiously out from among the display. With the exception of the heliotrope, all the plants in this box require a moderate amount of water. To ensure plentiful blooms, an average strength fertilizer is used on a continuous basis. Only the heliotrope needs to be deadheaded and must be checked to make sure that it is not drying out.

3 *Tagetes tenuifolia* 'Lulu' (signet marigold), 2 *Pelargonium peltatum* hybrids (geranium), 2 *Heliotropium arborescens* 'Marine' (heliotrope), 2 *Chrysanthemum multicaule* 'Kobold' (dwarf marguerite), 2 *Antirrhinum* hybrids (snapdragon).

Tobacco plants and *Scaevola aemula* form an ideal partnership here. One stretches upwards to flower, the other trails down to the ground, while the busy Lizzie cannot make up its mind which way to go. However, if the summer is a rainy one without much sunshine, the tobacco plant will stop blooming, and only the *Scaevola aemula* with its endless succession of flowers will prolong the summer display until well into autumn. All the plants in this box need plenty of water, so you will be kept busy with the watering can. If you do not have an automatic watering system, this box will in any case have a better chance of doing well in semi-shade.

**3** *Nicotiana sanderae* **'Nicki Red' (tobacco plant), 4** *Impatiens walleriana* **'Impuls Scharlachrot' (busy Lizzie), 4** *Scaevola aemula* **'Blue Wonder'.**

The begonias, with their blooms that glow like red-hot lava, can easily be seen from a distance and dominate the small-flowered lobelias and ageratum. The verbenas are more of a match for them and enhance the effect of the begonias.

**4 Begonia hybrids 'Nonstop Scharlach' (begonia), 3 Ageratum houstonianum 'Hawaii' (ageratum), 2 Verbena tenera 'Salome' (spreading verbena), 4 Lobelia erinus compacta 'Rosamunde' (lobelia).**

A multicoloured, cheerful mixture of flowers of different habit has been planted in this wooden box. In the back row stands the upright mealy sage together with the fuchsia 'Swingtime'. In the middle, the busy Lizzie has spread out a sea of blooms. The front row consists of the trailing fuchsia 'Red Spider', purple ageratum and white clouds of sweet alyssum.

**2 *Salvia farinacea* (mealy sage), 2 *Fuchsia* 'Swingtime' (fuchsia), 1 *Impatiens walleriana* 'Belizzy Rosa Stern' (busy Lizzie), 2 *Fuchsia* 'Red Spider' (fuchsia), 2 *Ageratum houstonianum* 'Atlantic' (ageratum). 2 *Lobularia maritima* 'Snow Crystals' (sweet alyssum).**

Everyone will be envious of this arrangement with its cheerful summer colours. The heliotrope was placed as a scented dominant plant in the background, flanked by two dazzling yellow calceolarias which contrast strongly with its dark purple blooms. The busy Lizzies with their orange-red flowers peep out of the dense foliage and form a transition to the trailing lobelias.

4 **Impatiens walleriana 'Accent Orange' (busy Lizzie), 2 Lobelia erinus pendula 'Sapphire' (lobelia), 2 Calceolaria integrifolia 'Goldari' (calceolaria), 3 Heliotropium arborescens 'Marine' (heliotrope).**

Scented heliotropes and colourful zinnias are the dominant plants in this combination, with the zinnias making an excellent transition to the underplanting. The lobelias hang over the edge of the box and benefit from the dappled shade cast by the other plants. This ensures that they do very well. Only the yellow marguerites do not get a chance in this grouping, with the other plants crowding them out. The busy Lizzies also have to make do with rather less space, but to compensate for this they are shaded by the zinnias from too much sun.

4 *Heliotropium arborescens* 'Mini Marine' (heliotrope), 2 *Chrysanthemum multicaule* 'Kobold' (marguerite), 3 *Zinnia angustifolia* 'Classic' (zinnia), 2 *Impatiens walleriana* 'Belizzy Rotstern' (busy Lizzie), 2 *Lobelia erinus compacta* 'Blauteppich' (lobelia).

This robust group brims over with flowers all summer long. The *Scaevola aemula* and *Melampodium paludosum* withstand rain just as well as they do a temporary heatwave. If you do forget to water the box and the *M. paludosum* wilts, it will soon be restored to life if you give it a good soaking.

3 **Chrysanthemum frutescens 'Vera'** (marguerite), 2 **Heliotropium arborescens 'Mini Marine'** (heliotrope), 4 **Nierembergia hippomanica 'Mont blanc'**, 2 **Melampodium paludosum 'Showstar'**, 2 **Scaevola aemula 'Blue Wonder'**.

A window box straight out of a fairy tale. The gently shimmering colours of this composition of summer flowers delight the viewer with their reticent, elegant charm. The begonias with their delicate pink blooms are obviously happy in this group. The sweet alyssum has snow-white flowers that frame the display to left and right. The verbena hangs down freely over the edge of the box, its pretty blooms mingling with the sweet alyssum and lobelia.

**4** *Begonia* **hybrids 'Nonstop Hellrosa' (begonia), 2** *Lobularia maritima* **'Snowdrift' (sweet alyssum), 2** *Verbena tenera* **'Kleopatra' (verbena), 2** *Lobelia erinus compacta* **'Cambridge Blue' (lobelia).**

In this small box, which is only 60 cm (24 inches) long, *Nierembergia* and *Centradenia* grow beneath the upright fuchsias and extend far over the edge of the box. Even the Indian pink, despite being cramped, manages to flower. Because these are all plants with similar requirements, none is crowded out and they combine to produce a harmonious blend of colours.

**1** *Fuchsia* **hybrid 'Beacon Rosa', 'Beacon' and 'Deutsche Perle' (fuchsia), 1** *Dianthus chinensis* **'Feuersturm' (Indian pink), 2** *Nierembergia hippomanica,* **1**

# *Plant combinations for containers in semi-shade*

| Upright | Semi-pendent | Trailing |
|---|---|---|
| | **WITH A HIGH NUTRIENT REQUIREMENT** | |
| *Chrysanthemum frutescens*<br>*Osteospermum ecklonis*<br>*Pelargonium zonale hybrids* | *Ageratum houstonianum*<br>*Lysimachia nummularia* | *Pelargonium peltatum hybrids*<br>*Plectranthus coleoides*<br>*Scaevola aemula* |
| | **WITH A MODERATE NUTRIENT REQUIREMENT** | |
| *Antirrhinum majus*<br>*Begonia*<br>*Fuchsia*<br>*Heliotropium arborescens*<br>*Mimulus* hybrids<br>*Nicotiana sanderae*<br>*Reseda odorata*<br>*Salvia farinacea*<br>*Tagetes* hybrids | *Begonia*<br>*Calceolaria integrifolia*<br>*Cuphea ignea*<br>*Diascia vigilis*<br>*Fuchsia*<br>*Impatiens*<br>*Lamium maculatum*<br>*Origanum vulgare* | *Begonia*<br>*Centradenia* 'Cascade'<br>*Fuchsia*<br>*Glechoma hederacea*<br>*Helichrysum petiolare*<br>*Lobelia erinus*<br>*Lobularia maritima*<br>*Mentha suaveolens*<br>*Monopsis lutea*<br>*Sutera diffusus*<br>*Tropaeolum majus* |
| | **WITH A LOW NUTRIENT REQUIREMENT** | |
| *Centaurea montana* | *Chrysanthemum multicaule*<br>*Tynophylla tenuiloba* | |

## PLANTING A WINDOW BOX:

In a box with two rows, the upright-growing summer plants are planted at the back, while the semi-pendent and trailing plants are alternated in the front. The semi-pendent plants prevent too sharp a demarcation occurring between the upright-growing and trailing plants by providing a link between them. Semi-pendent plants can also be used to good effect on their own with upright-growing plants. In a window box with space for just one row, it is best to plant upright-growing plants, semi-pendent and trailing plants alternately next to one other. *For more advice on combining plants, see page 79.*

## CLIMBING PLANTS SUITABLE FOR SEMI-SHADE:

*Aristolochia macrophylla*
*Clematis* hybrids
*Hedera helix*
*Lonicera*
*Parhenocissus* hybrids
*Phaseolus coccineus*
*Rhodochiton atrosanguineus*
*Tropaeolum peregrinum*

# The warm colours of autumn

Summer flowers do not fade so quickly in containers in semi-shade, but here too the display does come to an end. Autumn is drawing near, bringing with it a few more pretty flower compositions. As the autumn flowers on sale now are already fully grown, they only need to open all their blooms before using up all their strength after just a few weeks on display. You will also find plants suited to containers in semi-shade in the section on containers in full sun, page 86 onwards.

*The leaves of the staff vine glow in the yellow autumn sunlight, contributing to the Indian summer mood. All the summer flowers have already gone; only the* Bidens ferulifolia *in the hanging flowerpot carries bravely on producing its pretty yellow flowers until late into the autumn. The entire box is filled with autumn flowers bought from the market. The plants were bought fully grown and already in bud, and so could be crammed into the box to fill all the available space. Chrysanthemums, Hebe Andersonii hybrids, Senecio bicolor and feather grass provide a colourful spectacle. The perennial grasses are now at the height of their beauty and brighten up the atmosphere with their lively form. The dried seed heads were brought back from a walk for use as table decoration.*

# *Winter magic*

Christmas is not far off, and the container decorations put you in a festive mood. Little baubles hang from the fir and yew branches with their covering of hoar frost, and a gold-lacquered bow completes the arrangement. A medlar twig has been sprayed with gold and inserted in the front of the box. The wooden chair is also having a winter rest, for nobody will want to sit outdoors now!

If you do not have time to put together your own winter decoration, you could ask a florist to arrange your box tastefully for you.

*Even in winter, window boxes need not be empty but can be decorated with evergreen branches.*

# Containers in full shade

Containers in full shade do not need to have a dreary appearance; they too can have their own charm. With ferns, hydrangeas, foliage plants, grasses, busy Lizzies and fuchsias you can create expressive plantings.

You cannot do anything about the lighting conditions, but you can change the atmosphere. You can feel very comfortable on a patio or balcony in full shade and can make a little leafy paradise for yourself. So why not turn a dark, dreary north-facing area into a green oasis?

*Only tuberous begonias of the varieties 'Pin-Up' and 'Illumination' have been planted in this box, and then only those in shades of pink that will provide a harmonious overall impression. Even so, this design is not monotonous, for interest is supplied by the completely different flower shapes and habits of the begonias. The single-flowered, upright begonia variety 'Pin-Up' looks as if it were made of Meissen porcelain and towers on strong stems above the trailing begonias.*

An east- or west-facing patio or balcony can be in full shade because of a building opposite or large trees. In a north-facing situation, nature has imposed the shady conditions. In the heat of summer, with no direct sunlight, the air temperature is often mild, making it pleasant to be outside. It is therefore an ideal place to make yourself somewhere to sit among greenery. It is true that you do not have such a wide choice of plants for these lighting conditions, but you can achieve the same variety of colour even with fewer plant groups.

It is necessary to differentiate between shade-loving and shade-tolerant species. There are some plants that tolerate shade but, if they could choose, would prefer sun. In contrast, some flowers, such as busy Lizzies and fuchsias, love shade and do not thrive in sunshine where they would exhaust themselves too quickly. Begonias, busy Lizzies and fuchsias are available in an enormous range of colours. You will be able to put together some enchanting colour combinations using these species.

An arrangement in full shade even has some advantages over one in a sunny situation. Watering is not such a chore here, and the blooms are not over so quickly.

An all-season display has the most to offer in an area in full shade, and there are plenty of ideas for this in the chapter on the all-season display (page 154).

## Discreet blooms glow in the twilight

Even with containers in full shade, you can experience the thrill of the first flowers in spring.

Fully-grown harbingers of spring are bought from the nursery while in bud and planted in the boxes. The flowers will take time here to open fully, but they will last much longer than in a sunny situation. Summer bedding can therefore follow on immediately after the spring display comes to an end. When the spring flowers have finished blooming, you can plant the bulbs in the garden, because the lighting conditions on the patio or balcony are not sufficient to provide them with enough energy to ensure blooms again next year. You will find the portraits of bulbs that are suitable for containers in full shade from page 20 onwards.

*Here the sweetly scented Polyanthus daffodil 'Minnow' jostles for space with grape hyacinths. The yellow of the daffodils brings the spring sunshine on to the patio or balcony and contrasts well with the blue of the grape hyacinths.*

# Flower magic even in the shade

Locations in full shade are only suitable for spending long periods of time in at the height of summer, but they do allow you to enjoy some cool, fresh air, especially during the dog days. The plants available for the shaded area are fewer and less diverse, but this does not mean that it has to look boring and monotonous. Even in full shade, you can have containers overflowing with blooms if you select the right plants. There are no true summer flowers that require shade, but there is a fair number of flowering plants that will tolerate it.

The three large groups of plants that are most rewarding to grow in shade can be found on the following pages.

*Even in this setting you can be in close contact with nature. In the hanging box, busy Lizzies, begonias and fuchsias bring light to this summer retreat. On the floor are more boxes, each containing a different-coloured busy Lizzie. The* Hydrangea paniculata *has been grown as a standard and its white blooms create a further impression of light. When the area is tidied up for the winter, the hydrangea alone remains standing there in its tub, which must of course be insulated against frost.*

113

*In this 60 cm (24 inch) box, the busy Lizzies provide a continuous profusion of flowers all summer long. Even in a shady place, they need regular applications of fertilizer to maintain this high performance. On the left and right, two* Impatiens walleriana *have been planted and they soon filled the box with their flowers and leaves. Crowning them in the middle is an* Impatiens New Guinea *hybrid, which is of more upright habit. Below them, the fuchsia lets its bell-shaped flowers trail downwards like garlands.*

---

**2 *Impatiens walleriana* hybrids (busy Lizzies), 1 *Impatiens* New Guinea hybrid (busy Lizzie), 1 *Fuchsia* 'Pink Ballet Girl' (fuchsia).**

---

*Many individual plants suited to shady conditions liven up this setting and lend it character. In the box is the begonia 'Pin-Up' in full glory. Its blooms could easily compete with those of an orchid for beauty and elegance. The busy Lizzies carry on flowering industriously in the shade. The cactus dahlia was added as a fully-grown pot plant. The* Acalypha indica *normally lives indoors, but can be outside in the fresh air in summer. On the floor are fuchsias and begonias.*

---

**2 *Begonia semperflorens* hybrids (begonia), 4 *Begonia* hybrids 'Pin-Up' (begonia), 2 *Impatiens walleriana* (busy Lizzie), 2 *Dahlia* hybrids (dahlia), 1 *Acalypha indica*, 1 *Fuchsia* hybrid (fuchsia), 1 *Aristolochia macrophylla* (Dutchman's pipe).**

---

Golden orange tuberous begonias and orange-red busy Lizzies bring warmth into the cool shade and make an eye-catching display even from afar. The tuberous begonias in the back row have single and double blooms. The cheerful busy Lizzies with white star markings were planted in front of the upright begonias so that they could spread out unhindered over the front of the box. They should not be planted too closely so as to avoid cramping the busy Lizzies' urge to spread out. They quickly take the lead and will soon crowd out any other plants in the box. The lobelias that were intended to round off the box at each end are already under attack, and the treasure flowers in the middle dream of a sunny position in which they would flourish much more readily.

With the begonia cultivar 'Charisma Orange' you could start an orange-red fire of blooms on your shady setting that could easily be seen from a distance. Actually, Elatior begonias are typical house plants that bloom without a break all summer long. The cultivar 'Charisma Orange' now gives you one that is suitable for growing outdoors. It is less prone to breaking in strong winds and is also easier to grow than tuberous begonias. However, since it does not have a tuber, it cannot be overwintered. None of the begonias like either being waterlogged or drying out, so the plants should be kept moderately damp.

---

**5** *Begonia eliator* **hybrids 'Charisma Orange' (begonia).**

---

**4** *Begonia* **hybrids 'Nonstop Gold-orange' (begonia), 2** *Lobelia erinus compacta* **'Blue Moon' (lobelia), 1** *Gazania* **hybrid 'Czardas Weiß' (treasure flower), 2** *Impatiens walleriana* **'Accent Orange Star' (busy Lizzie).**

## *Impatiens walleriana*

(Busy Lizzie)

Busy Lizzies used to be exclusively kept as house plants. The somewhat spindly-looking plants were regarded as old-fashioned and were out of favour for a long time. However, plant breeders have been busy and from the house plant they have developed an outstanding patio plant of compact habit for growing in semi-shade and shade. Busy Lizzies even bloom in dark corners where almost nothing else will. They come in so many colours that it would be possible to have a complete display using this species alone. Being a tropical plant, busy Lizzies grow vigorously and need to be planted at least 30 cm (12 inches) from their neighbours if they are to develop fully. They look even more attractive when combined with other summer flowers. However, you should use just two busy Lizzies at most in a mixed planting because of their need to spread out. After only a few weeks they will have settled in and will bloom without a break until autumn. If you give them too little space, they have to grow upwards and then will break easily. If you put a vigorous-growing plant behind, they will grow forwards. They will then hang half over the edge of the box in a very attractive way. Because of their dominant habit, busy Lizzies should never be planted at the back because they will suppress and even overgrow the plants in front.

Because they are easy to grow, busy Lizzies are highly recommended for newcomers to container gardening. It does not

*Double blooms:* Impatiens *'Rosette'.*

take long before you get results with them. The colour range goes from white through pink, red and purple to two-colour varieties. They are semi-pendent in habit and are therefore very useful as hanging flowerpot plants. The double-bloomed varieties are also enchanting and could almost compete with roses for charm.

**SITUATION:** semi-shade to dappled shade.

**COMPOST:** John Innes No. 2 or equivalent.

**CARE:** Busy Lizzies love damp, cool conditions and their blooms will withstand rain. They soon wilt if allowed to dry out. Watering and a continuous supply of fertilizer are essential if they are to produce a magnificent display. The fertilizer should not have too high a nitrogen content, otherwise all the plants' strength will go into the leaves instead of into the flowers. If the compost

is kept damp, the plants will rarely be troubled by pests. Deadheading is not necessary since they have good powers of regeneration.

**PROPAGATION:** if you have fallen in love with a particular variety and want to be certain that it will bloom again next year, you must take cuttings from your favourite plant in the autumn when you tidy up for the winter. Place the little cuttings in a glass of water until they have formed plenty of roots. Pot them up and put them on a windowsill where the temperature is 10-15°C (50-59°F).

**OVERWINTERING:** possible, but not recommended.

**IN A BOX:** pages 10, 47, 51, 73, 92, 100, 101, 102, 109, 112, 114, 116, 179.

Impatiens New Guinea *hybrids*.

*Busy Lizzie makes a
good hanging basket
subject.*

### *Impatiens New Guinea* hybrids

These busy Lizzies differ from *Impatiens walleriana* in that they have larger blooms and often have leaves of a greenish-red. They are also of upright habit. *Impatiens New Guinea* hybrids need plenty of warmth, and so just how well they develop depends on the weather. During a hot summer they grow to small bushes and are covered in large, brilliantly-coloured flowers. However, if the summer is wet and cold, they refuse to grow. From the large range of varieties, the compact-growing ones are the most suitable for planting in boxes, and the taller varieties can develop more attractively when planted on their own, enabling them to stretch out their decorative foliage on all sides.

In a mixed box they are the dominant plants. An attractive progression can be created by combining New Guinea hybrids with, for example, trailing fuchsias, cigar flowers or their smaller relatives (*I. walleriana*) as underplanting.

**SITUATION:** warm, sheltered semi-shade (ideally an east-facing position).

**COMPOST:** John Innes No. 2 or equivalent.

**CARE:** all busy Lizzies are very thirsty. Regular feeding and watering is an absolute must.

**PROPAGATION:** by cuttings in late summer or early spring. By seed in March.

**OVERWINTERING:** only appropriate for rooted cuttings under light and moderately warm conditions (5°C).

**IN A BOX:** page 114.

Fuchsia
'Viva Ireland'

**SITUATION:** Fuchsias are natives of the cool mountain regions of Central and South America where they grow in light, humus-rich soil in the dappled shade of trees. With the exception of the sun-loving *Triphylla* hybrids, fuchsias need a cool situation in semi-shade or full shade, preferably with high humidity. They are best suited to east- and north-facing areas.

Fuchsia *'Swingtime' (top) and 'Dark Eyes' (bottom).*

## *Fuchsia* hybrids
(Fuchsia)

It can be rightly said of fuchsias that they are among the most beautiful and rewarding flowers for shady conditions. From May until late autumn they are the stars of the container in full shade with their single and double blooms. Fuchsias can be divided into three groups according to their growth habit:

### 1. Vigorous plants of upright or lax habit.
These are best suited to the larger area. They make excellent standards. Since standards with their heavy crowns are very prone to wind damage, they require good support.

### 2. Slow-growing plants of upright habit.
These varieties are excellent for small settings and as dominant plants in a box combination.

### 3. Trailing varieties
Plant these fuchsias at the edge of the box so that they can trail down to their full length. They will also grow into magnificent hanging basket specimens.

Never buy fuchsias in full bloom, but go for young plants that are in bud or just coming into flower.

**COMPOST:** John Innes No. 2 or equivalent.

**CARE:** feed fuchsias regularly with liquid fertilizer to keep them in the mood for flowering. Fuchsias are the only summer flowers which like having their leaves sprinkled with water when you give them their evening drink. If you do not want them to stop flowering for a while, you will have to deadhead constantly. For a fuchsia lover this is not a chore but a joy. 'Cascade' and 'Gesäuseperle' are two cultivars that will continue flowering reliably with little care. However, fuchsias are liable to be troubled by aphids and whitefly, and by red spider mite in hot, dry weather.

**PROPAGATION:** by cuttings in August.

**OVERWINTERING:** in a light, cool room (5°C) if you want to keep the foliage. They can also be overwintered in a dark cellar, but they will then lose all their leaves and flower later the following year. In spring the plants are cut back to two-thirds their size. The root ball must not be allowed to dry out during the winter, but give it only a very little water.

**IN A BOX:** page 92, 101, 104, 112, 114, 164.

*A setting full of fuchsias, surrounded by green-leafed foliage plants.*

## *Begonia* hybrids

(Tuberous begonia)

The tuberous begonias represent a large group of plants with many forms and colours that are suited to full shade.

On sale you will find large and small-flowered, double and single, erect and creeping varieties in many shades of the warm colours yellow, orange, red and pink. The begonia can scarcely be surpassed by any other plant in terms of abundance and brilliance of blooms. So if you love vivid colours, you cannot go wrong with begonias. But the begonia range also offers delicate pastel shades for those who prefer subdued colours. For romantics there is the single-flowered, delicate pink cultivar 'Pin-Up' with its simple but effective elegance.

The cane-stemmed upright begonias are unfortunately fairly prone to wind damage. They are therefore unsuitable for a wind-swept display. However, the blooms of all begonias are strikingly rain-resistant. The heavy blooms pull the otherwise upright-growing stems strongly downwards so that they droop slightly over the edge of the box. The trailing begonias *(Begonia pendula* hybrids) represent a special group of tuberous begonias with thinner, supple shoots that trail right down over the edge of the box. An improved form of the trailing begonia is the 'garland' begonia 'Illumination Zartrosa' which is the best for use in hanging arrangements.

**SITUATION:** semi-shade to shade.
**COMPOST:** John Innes No. 2 or equivalent.
**CARE:** water regularly, the compost should never be allowed to dry out. Begonias bloom from May until October.
**PROPAGATION:** by division of the tubers after forcing in early spring.
**OVERWINTERING:** if the begonia tubers are to be overwintered, you will have to leave the plants to mature until late autumn. During this stage of development they only need a little water. They are then taken out of the compost and stored, wrapped in newspaper, in a dry place.
Tuberous begonias that you have bought from the nursery in full bloom are generally young plants

grown from seed. So do not worry if these begonias have not yet grown large tubers. Small tubers can of course be overwintered, but they will not produce such luxuriant blooms the following year. The tubers will grow larger year by year. As an alternative you could buy a large tuber in early spring and force it on the windowsill

*Begonias bloom tirelessly even in the shade (above and left).*

at 20°C (68°F). If the tubers are very dry, they will need to be soaked for an hour in lukewarm water. You can then plant them in compost, taking care that the 'dent' (where the shoot will emerge) is uppermost.
**IN A BOX:** pages 101, 104, 108, 112, 114, 116, 179.

### *Begonia eliator* hybrids

The begonias in this group are in fact typical houseplants. 'Charisma' is a hybrid that is excellently suited to the patio or balcony. The plants produce blooms in intense shades of orange. They are of compact habit and flower tirelessly all summer long.
In contrast to the tuberous begonia, this group does not form tubers and can therefore not be overwintered. If the plants are allowed to become too dry, they easily fall prey to mildew.
**IN A BOX:** pages 96, 117.

### *Begonia semperflorens* hybrids

The undemanding *semperflorens* hybrids are suited both to sun and to semi-shade. There are varieties with light or dark foliage that bear pinkish-red, orange or red blooms.
A native of Brazil, this begonia grows to about 15 cm (6 inches) high and is very resistant to the effects of weather. The flowers and leaves shine as if they were coated with wax. The plants are very sensitive to frost and are damaged even at 0°C (32°F). They go well with ageratum and white dwarf chrysanthemums.
**IN A BOX:** pages 164, 179.

## *Hydrangea*
(Hydrangea)

A native of south-east Asia, this shrub with the ball-shaped flower heads is universally popular. It is very robust and blooms from May until well into August. The common hydrangea can grow to a height of 1-2 metres (3-6 feet) and has outstretched branches. You can often obtain standards, and these are of course particularly suited to the patio because they save space. They are available in many colours from white through pink and red to blue. The colour is also dependent on the type of compost, for acid soil leads to the majority of flowers being bluish, while alkaline soil will give them a reddish colour. If pink-flowering hydrangeas are watered with a solution of alum (from a garden centre) in water, the flowers will gradually turn blue.

Only the colour white cannot be influenced by the pH value. The flower heads are fascinating because the colour of the petals varies with the age of the blooms. This characteristic inspires florists to weave pretty garlands from them. *Hydrangea macrophylla* 'Hortensia' (common hydrangea) is a perennial woody plant and should be overwintered. *H. paniculata* 'Grandiflora' produces large white paniculate inflorescences which become tinged with pink as they fade. It only flowers from July until August. Standards are also very attractive.

**SITUATION:** shady and sheltered from wind (standards are at risk).

**COMPOST:** John Innes No. 2 or equivalent, acid pH.

**CARE:** in summer it needs plenty of water but will not tolerate waterlogging. To prevent mildew you must take care that the leaves do not get too wet. Feed every two weeks. The leaves turn yellow under the influence of chalky soil. Susceptible to mildew. *H. paniculata* is prone to developing yellow leaves (chlorosis), but the veins remain green.

**OVERWINTERING:** before the first frosts, bring the plant indoors and keep in a cool place. If it is in the dark, the plant must be moved to a light, cool place in March as its growth starts early in the spring.

**IN A BOX:** pages 6, 93, 112.

*The common hydrangea makes an elegant subject.*

*Abutilon flowers over a long period.*

## *Abutilon* hybrids
(Abutilon)

This is a well-known and popular house and container plant. Its bell-shaped flowers grace the display tirelessly in summer and are available in white, yellow, orange and red. The maple-like leaves are generally green, but there are also varieties with variegated leaves. Most abutilons grow upwards and can easily be grown as standards. *Abutilon megapotamicum* is the only one to make an excellent hanging basket plant since it has pendent branches. Its flowers are somewhat smaller and lantern-shaped. If the leaves turn yellow and drop off, the root ball has dried out in the heat – you must make sure this does not happen. A special feature of the abutilon is its cleanliness. The flowers drop to the ground when over and only need to be swept up.

**SITUATION:** semi-shade to light shade. The variegated kinds will also tolerate full sun if watered well.

**COMPOST:** John Innes No. 2 or equivalent.

**CARE:** water copiously. Faded blooms fall off by themselves.

**PROPAGATION:** by cuttings in spring.

**OVERWINTERING:** it is easy to overwinter abutilons since all you need do is cut them back vigorously and bring them into a warm room. After a short recovery period they will continue flowering indoors – this behaviour is typical of a plant with a long flowering period.

**IN A BOX:** pages 33, 93.

### Glechoma hederacea 'Variegata'

(Variegated ground ivy)

The native wild form of this Eurasian plant grows on humus-rich soil and has bluish-violet flowers. This particular cultivar for situations in semi-shade or shade has white and green variegated, aromatic leaves and is used to give variety of texture. In the shade, ground ivy provides an accompaniment to busy Lizzies and fuchsias just as *Plectranthus forsteri* does to geraniums in full sun. It forms long shoots that grow vertically downwards from the container. Where the leaves grow out of the stem, roots soon start to grow on contact with soil. The shoots can attain 2 metres (6 feet) in length if the plant is suitably fed.

It also looks very attractive alone as a hanging flowerpot plant.

**SITUATION:** semi-shade to shade.

**COMPOST:** John Innes No. 2 or equivalent.

**CARE:** growth depends on the amount of fertilizer and water given.

**OVERWINTERING:** this hardy herbaceous perennial can be overwintered out of doors without any problems. In areas where the winter is especially harsh, insulating the root ball is recommended.

**IN A BOX:** page 43.

*Ground ivy makes a good foliage plant.*

*Silvery foliage is provided by the dead-nettle.*

### Lamium maculatum 'White Nancy'

(Dead-nettle)

This variegated form of the native dead-nettle is an ideal accompaniment to fuchsias or begonias. A hardy, silvery-leaved herbaceous perennial, it quickly provides ground cover and then grows elegantly over the edge of the container. The dead-nettle's bright carpet of leaves brings a cheerful note even to shady positions. In summer, snow-white hooded flowers appear on upright stalks to give even more variety to the planting.

**SITUATION:** semi-shade to shade.

**COMPOST:** John Innes No. 2 or equivalent.

**CARE:** undemanding.

**PROPAGATION:** by cuttings.

**IN A BOX:** page 179.

# A long, golden autumn

In this display, autumn can be seen to best advantage. Asters, dahlias, ornamental cabbage and grasses bring colour and an autumnal mood to the area in full shade. All the plants were bought fully grown, either in bud or in bloom. Autumn on the north-facing patio or balcony remains colourful for a few days longer since the flowers take longer to fade when not exposed to sunshine.

Unfortunately the grasses cannot stay here because they need more light in order to grow. In the box, the last blooms of the fuchsia and *Bacopa* remain from summer. The *Acalypha* merrily dangles its cat's tails from the hanging flower pot. A typical house plant, the *Acalypha* will have to be brought indoors before the first frost.

*An attractively simple planting in an old orange box*

# Long-lasting winter decorations

When the leaves have fallen, the container gardener can finally sit down in a comfortable armchair for a well-earned winter rest. An exciting, flower-filled year in close contact with nature is finally over and now is the time to reflect on it in peace and quiet. However, if you do not want to look out all winter long on a sad and deserted area, you can fill it with the kinds of greenery a florist might use, as well as decorative accessories.

Twigs and seed heads brought back from a country walk have been prettily arranged in the box and will fulfil their role until spring. The box branches form a small green hedge in the background and provide an excellent backdrop against which the frost-resistant terracotta ornaments stand out beautifully. The knarled roots were brought back from a walk in the woods and round off the picture with their bizarre shapes.

# Container ideas

## A cottage garden on the patio or balcony

If you have fallen in love with cottage gardens you can easily recreate some aspects of your own. In a real cottage garden, vegetables, herbs and fruit are grown alongside many summer flowers. Vegetables and herbs keep the kitchen supplied and summer flowers provide a feast for the eyes. You cannot have more variety and colour than on a cottage garden patio. The message quickly gets round in the insect world about where there is a nectar-rich patch of green to be found. Butterflies, bees and bumble bees will soon pay you a visit. Typical summer flowers for the display are *Tagetes,* sweet peas and pot marigolds.

*Here everything is growing together peacefully side by side. A cottage garden would just not be the same without sunflowers. It is a bit much to expect that you would be able to survive on what you grow in your containers, but it will certainly be able to provide a culinary treat now and then.*

## *Fresh produce from a container box*

Most kinds of vegetable require at least a few hours' full sun a day, which is what they will usually get in a container in semi-shade. You will soon have success with radishes, runner beans, cucumbers, onions, tomatoes and lettuce. Then you may like to try the more difficult types of vegetable. If your containers are on a balcony, you will not have to worry about snails invading and destroying all your young plants. Plant breeders have already developed suitable varieties for the balcony garden. They generally remain small, but nevertheless produce good yields. For example, cherry tomatoes are particularly suitable and also have a very good flavour.

*An organic garden on two levels in a very small space.*

Even lettuces grow exceptionally well in containers and, as you can pick them just before eating, you can enjoy them while they are crisp and fresh. The cut-and-come-again varieties are especially to be recommended since the leaves grow again. Scarlet runner beans are very useful, transforming the area into a green arbour and providing privacy. They have bright red flowers and give you a feast of bean pods in late summer that are delicious when harvested young. Runner beans are sown at the end of May where they are to be grown. Almost all types of vegetable need containers at least 20-30 cm (8-12 inches) in depth.

*Home-grown cucumbers, tomatoes and peppers alongside summer flowers.*

# A herb garden on a small scale

As anyone who appreciates culinary pleasures knows, fresh herbs are an essential flavouring for many dishes. A sunny area is perfectly suited to growing herbs.

However, if they are to develop their full aroma, they need a sheltered location in full sun. There, even herbs such as basil, savory and thyme, that are difficult to grow, will thrive since they need plenty of sun and warmth.

To save space, pots can be arranged on staggered shelving. Herbs will even flourish when planted close together in a container out of the wind.

The aromatic leaves must be harvested before all their strength has been used up in flowering. Cut down the plant before it flowers and hang it upside down to dry in a shady, airy place. That way the aroma will be preserved for a long time.

In **containers in semi-shade** you can grow hardy, native herbs such as chives, parsley, burnet saxifrage and chervil.

In **containers in full shade** you can only plant cress, borage and lettuces.

Borage, tarragon and lovage require a high amount of nutrients, while marjoram, oregano, rosemary, sage, thyme and wormwood prefer light soil and a low amount of nutrients. Most other herbs require a moderate amount of nutrients and will grow in normal compost.

*A sunny situation is ideal for fresh herbs to grow and flourish.*

# Fruit in Containers

If you like eating summer fruits, you can plant raspberries, strawberries, currants and blackberries in tubs and boxes. You will not get such a large harvest as from a garden, but you will be able to eat fruit that is just as fresh and you will certainly have enough to make a vitamin-rich muesli. These little delicacies will just melt on your tongue. There are even miniature apple and pear trees that are suitable for containers. Despite their small size, they still bear plenty of fruit.

*Strawberries from pot to mouth!*
*Below: blackberries.*

# Summer-flowering climbing plants for a perfect display

If you would like to create living walls of flowers and leaves on your patio and you only have a small one, you should go for annual climbers. These do not need such large pots as their longer-lived colleagues to fuel their twining, coiling and climbing, and will generally provide you with masses of flowers all summer long.

The green walls will protect you from light breezes and nosy neighbours.

If you combine climbing plants and summer flowers you will create some charming contrasts. Plant the climbers at the back of a large container and a pretty group of summer flowers at the front. The climbing plants will then form a background to set off the colours of the summer flowers. Most annual climbers are natives of the south and need south- or east-facing situations if they are to do well in a northern climate.

If you want to make your setting private, you will need climbers with dense foliage such as *Ipomoea lobata* (Spanish flag), scarlet runner beans or the cup-and-saucer vine.

An important climbing plant is the bottle gourd which soon covers the walls with its large leaves. It is a real vertical take-off specialist that will even supply any overhead balcony with leaves if its pot is large enough. In autumn, the bottle-shaped fruits are formed and hang like clubs. Climbing plants also look pretty if you push a few bamboo canes wigwam-fashion into a pot and let the plants climb up them.

In exposed situations, climbers will need protection from the wind in the form of straw matting or sail cloth as they start to grow. This is then removed as soon as they have got a strong hold. Do not forget to harvest a few seeds in autumn to sow again next year.

The first frosts will put an end to this 'high-flying' and the dying plants will have to be removed.

**Plants to provide privacy:**
Height: 2-3 metres (6-10 feet): *Cobaea scandens* (cup-and-saucer vine), *Ipomoea lobata* (Spanish flag), *Asarina erubescens* (creeping gloxinia), *Phaeseolus coccineus* (scarlet runner bean)

**Decorative climbing plants:**
Height: 1-1.50 metres (3-5 feet): *Thunbergia alata* (Black-eyed Susan), *Lathyrus, Asarina barclaiana*

*Man and dog feel good in this arbour of annual climbing plants.*

## *Lathyrus odoratus*

(Sweet pea)

If you have ever had the pleasantly scented sweet pea in your display, you will never want to be without it again. Sweet peas are available in all the summer colours of white, pink, red and purple, with the two-coloured varieties being just as attractive as the plain varieties. The vigorous sweet pea can climb as much as 2 metres (6 feet) high and can provide privacy as well as scent. It has to be placed in a pot on the floor since it would climb up too high if planted in a window box.

For containers, the cultivar 'Super Snoop' is ideal. It grows to 40 cm (16 inches) and does not need any support. The cultivar 'Little Sweetheart' only grows 25 cm (10 inches) high and comes in a mixture of colours.

**Situation:** this beautiful Italian flower loves hot sunshine but will not tolerate strong winds. A particularly enchanting colour combination can be created with pink sweet peas and brilliant pale blue morning glory.

**COMPOST:** John Innes No. 1 or equivalent.

**CARE:** sweet peas need regular feeding with low doses of fertilizer. They are very sensitive to overfeeding and will quickly develop yellow leaves. Since they love humus-rich, well-drained compost, it is advisable to provide drainage. Because the compost becomes exhausted, it must be changed annually if sweet peas are to be grown again in the same pot each time. If their roots remain in cold water for too long, the leaves turn yellow and flowers are no longer produced.

**PROPAGATION:** from May onwards sweet peas can be sown directly in the boxes since they are not frost-tender. The seeds are buried individually 2 cm (1 inch) deep at intervals of 5-10 cm (2-4 inches).

## *Ipomoea*

(Morning glory)

These extremely robust and vigorous climbers open new, magnificently coloured, funnel-shaped flowers every morning. Every single bloom is impressive in its brilliance. They are ideal climbers for east-facing areas, but if you want to enjoy the blooms at their best, you have to be an early riser, for they open as soon as the sun is up.

*Sweet pea and morning glory.*

By midday they are already wilting and next morning new flowers will open. A strikingly beautiful variety is 'Himmelblau' with brilliant, steel-blue, funnel-shaped flowers. *Ipomoea purpurea* has heart-shaped leaves and the flowers come in shades of red, purple and blue. A close relative, *Pharbitis learii,* has three-lobed leaves. Every morning it opens its large, dark-blue, funnel-shaped flowers that are grouped together in clumps. It can only be propagated by cuttings.

If you give the plants a support made from bamboo canes or willow twigs, they will twine themselves comfortably around it as they grow upwards.

**SITUATION:** sunny, but sheltered from the wind.

**COMPOST:** John Innes No. 2 or equivalent.

**CARE:** undemanding.

**PROPAGATION:** by seed. From March onwards these plants are easy to grow from seed. The hard seed cases must be soaked beforehand in warm water. After mid-May they can be sown outdoors directly where they are to grow.

*The blooms of the passion flower.*

## *Passiflora* hybrids
(Passion flower)

The passion flower was brought back from the Brazilian rain forest by monks in the 17th century. They saw in the flower a symbol of Jesus' Passion and accordingly named it Passiflora *(passio =* Passion, *flor =* flower). The most commonly available kind is *Passiflora caerulea,* which is sold in winter as a house plant for south-facing windowsills. These vigorous climbers should be set free in spring and planted in a large tub so that they can climb up a trellis against the warm wall of the house. The blooms will then be produced from spring until autumn.

**SITUATION:** sunny.

**COMPOST:** John Innes No. 3 or equivalent.

**CARE:** regular watering and feeding are necessary, but the plants will not tolerate waterlogging.

**PROPAGATION:** by cuttings, but you get results more quickly if you buy a passion flower as a house plant early in the year.

**OVERWINTERING:** in mild areas it is possible to overwinter the passion flower in the container if you release the plant from the trellis, roll and wrap it up, and provide insulation for the root ball. Otherwise the plant can spend the winter in a cool cellar or other dark place.

*A plant that quickly provides privacy:* Ipomoea lobata *(Spanish flag).*

## *Ipomoea lobata*
(Spanish flag)

If you need a plant to provide you rapidly with privacy for the summer, *Ipomoea lobata* is the one for you. Its inflorescences are particularly striking – the buds are a dazzling red, then change to orange, and the flowers, when open, are pale yellow in colour. *Ipomoea lobata* has amazing powers of growth. In warm summers it easily reaches 4-5 metres (13-16 feet) in height and is therefore one of the best annual climbers for providing privacy.

To be able to grow like this, the plant needs a large container and a trellis to twine itself around.
**SITUATION:** sunny and sheltered from wind.
**COMPOST:** John Innes No. 2 or equivalent, humus-rich, light compost rich in minerals (mix in sand). It is advisable to provide drainage.
**CARE:** water regularly. This plant will not tolerate waterlogging.
**PROPAGATION:** by seed from March to May on the windowsill.

*A decorative climber: black-eyed Susan.*

### Thunbergia alata

(Black-eyed Susan)

Black-eyed Susan does not have any tendrils with which to pull itself upwards. If you want it to cover a trellis with greenery, you will have to attach the shoots as they grow. In June, the typical brilliant yellow flowers appear with their funnel-shaped black 'eye' in the centre. This plant is particularly rewarding when grown on a white or heat-retaining wall and will clad the dull walls of a house in living colour. Black-eyed Susan is also available with white petals and a black centre. A particularly attractive display can be created by growing both varieties in one box. It can also make a beautiful hanging basket subject.
**SITUATION:** full sun, sheltered from the wind.
**COMPOST:** John Innes No. 2 or equivalent compost containing lime and plenty of nutrients.
**CARE:** water regularly. If you want the young plant to grow more branches, you will have to cut it back once.
**PROPAGATION:** by seed at the end of March.

### Phaseolus coccineus

(Scarlet runner bean)

The scarlet runner bean is an extremely fast climber and soon transforms the patio or balcony into a bower. It is both decorative and useful. Provide wire or string supports so that it can climb upwards.
Its abundant scarlet

*Attractive and useful: the scarlet runner bean.*

papilionaceous flowers are followed by quantities of delicious beans in July. When grown in containers they can reach a height of 3 metres (10 feet) and produce just as big a vegetable crop as in a garden.
**SITUATION:** sun to semi-shade.
**COMPOST:** John Innes No. 3 or equivalent.
**CARE:** make sure the plants have sufficient water when in flower. If they remain dry for too long, the leaves will drop off. When training the shoots, you should remember that the bean plant twines its stems in an anticlockwise direction.
**PROPAGATION:** by seed in the boxes where they are to grow from late May to early July.
**OVERWINTERING:** allow the pods to ripen and sow the seeds next spring.

*The cup-and-saucer vine has red leaves in autumn.*

## Cobaea scandens

(Cup-and-saucer vine)

This vigorous grower soon covers walls and trellises. At the end of July it begins to produce flowers and continues flowering until autumn without a break. The leaves turn dark red in autumn.
**SITUATION:** warm and sheltered.
**COMPOST:** John Innes No. 2, humus-rich and well-drained.
**CARE:** if the cup-and-saucer vine is to make a dense wall of leaves, it must be planted in a suitably large container. The shoots must be trained up the trellis. Give a moderate amount of fertilizer at first, then reduce the quantity from July onwards.
**PROPAGATION:** in March on the windowsill. Cup-and-saucer vines are sensitive to cold and must be gradually accustomed to outdoor conditions. Place the pots outdoors on frost-free days and bring them in again in the evening. They can finally be left outside permanently from the end of May.

Asarina barclaiana.

## Asarina barclaiana

The *Asarina* is a native of Mexico and is grown in Europe as an annual climbing plant that produces pretty blue, red and purple flowers. In only one season it grows to 1-1.5 metres (3-5 feet) high in a container and forms dense foliage. It is not particularly suitable for providing privacy but makes a decorative hanging flowerpot plant. Its large-flowering relative, *Asarina erubescens* (creeping gloxinia), makes a better screen since it covers walls very rapidly with its large leaves and gives a good degree of privacy.
**SITUATION:** sunny and sheltered.
**COMPOST:** John Innes No. 2 or equivalent.
**CARE:** undemanding.
**PROPAGATION:** by seed on the windowsill in March.

*A hanging scented garden.*

# *A potpourri for connoisseurs: scented plants*

The dream of surrounding yourself with pleasant fragrances can be realized even in the smallest area. By growing plants with scented blooms and leaves, the setting can easily be given a completely new dimension. Let yourself be transported into the realm of plant fragrances and allow them to enchant you. The scent of most flowering plants is at its peak as the day draws to a close and the time for relaxation begins. It is not only people who are attracted by the scent of

flowers – the insect world finds them irresistible, and butterflies, bees, bumble bees and moths will visit your display.

*The freshly scented orange blossom has already given way to miniature fruits. Now it is the turn of the lilies, lavender and herbs to spread their fragrance over the entire display.*

Through the year with scented plants and leaves:

**Spring:**

*Cheiranthus cheiri*
*Clematis*
*Convallaria majalis*
*Galanthus nivalis*
*Hyacinthus orientalis*
*Iris reticulata*
*Lonicera caprifolium*
*Narcissus* hybrids
*Viola odorata*

**Summer to autumn:**

*Anthemis nobilis*
*Chrysanthemum parthenium*
*Citrus*
*Datura suaveolens*
*Dianthus caryophyllus*
*Heliotropium*
*Lathyrus odorata*
*Lavandula*
*Lilium* hybrids
*Matthiola incana*
*Mentha piperita*
*Mirabilis jalapa*
*Myrtus communis*
*Nerium oleander*
*Pelargonium*
*Petunia* hybrids
*Plectranthus forsteri*
*Reseda odorata*
*Rosa* hybrids
*Rosmarinus officinalis*
*Salvia sclarea*
*Solanum rantonnetii*
*Thymus citriodorus*
*Thymus serpyllum*
*Tropaeolum majus*

*The four o'clock flower opens its blooms in the afternoon.*

### *Mirabilis jalapa*

(Four o'clock flower)

This exquisite delicately scented flower only opens its blooms around four o'clock in the afternoon, hence its name. As the humidity rises, it imparts its powerful, fruity scent to attract hordes of moths. It is just the plant for the container owner to enjoy at the end of the working day. A bushy plant growing to

about 50 cm (20 inches) high, it can fill half a container by itself, so the best way is to plant it on its own in a pot. The special characteristic of this plant is that in the wild there are specimens with white, yellow, deep pink or red flowers. It can even happen that there are flowers of different colours on one and the same plant. Collect the seeds once they have formed in summer so that

you will be able to sow this charming scented plant again next year.

**SITUATION:** full sun.

**COMPOST:** John Innes No. 2 or equivalent.

**CARE:** this plant requires a normal amount of water and regular feeding.

**PROPAGATION:** by seed in April.

## Matthiola incana

(Stock, gillyflower)

Stocks are familiar to many garden lovers because of their captivating scent. Single-flowered varieties in particular are intensely fragrant. The scent is at its most powerful in the evening – just when you come home from work. Varieties with double blooms are the best for the container since they do not set seed so quickly and so remain in flower for longer. They are available in many romantic pastel shades from creamy white to crimson and purple. Among seeds for double-flowered stocks there is always a proportion that grow into single-flowered plants. You can recognize these seedlings by their dark leaves and weed them out if necessary. Stocks also last remarkably well as cut flowers, filling the whole room with their captivating scent for up to two weeks.

**SITUATION:** sunny.

**COMPOST:** John Innes No. 2 or equivalent.

**CARE:** feed and water regularly.

**PROPAGATION:** by seed in March/April on the windowsill.

*Intensely scented stocks.*

## Reseda odorata

(Mignonette)

The unspectacular mignonette has long been neglected, but it has a definite place on the scented display. Its overhanging habit makes it very well suited for use as underplanting in boxes. The scent blends very well with that of summer-flowering stocks which can also be planted in the same box. Mignonette also goes very well beneath a scented rose. A well-known variety is 'Grandiflorum' with white flowers and red anthers. Its unspectacular, greenish-yellow clusters of flowers have a scent like that of violets which will hold you in its spell. Mignonette really comes into its own in a container since you can position it on a level with your nose. People may like or dislike certain fragrances, but surely nobody can dislike the scent of the mignonette. Bees love it, and will certainly visit

your display. Every time a flower is touched during the day it says thank you with a cloud of fruity scent. In the evening, the flowers impart their scent by themselves. They will also last for several days in a vase, filling the room with their fragrance.

**SITUATION:** sun to semi-shade.

**COMPOST:** John Innes No. 1 or equivalent loamy compost.

**CARE:** pinch out the tips of the young plants to encourage a bushy shape. They do not like being too damp because in their native North Africa they live in rock crevices and on grassy slopes.

**PROPAGATION:** it is possible to sow seed directly where the plants are to grow, but this is not always successful. It is better to start the seed off in small pots.

*Mignonette has a scent of violets.*

# A legacy for the next generation

Give your children the opportunity to be in close contact with nature even in a town. They will learn all sorts of things, including where tomatoes come from! In gardens, children are usually given their own corner where they can find out if they have green fingers. On the patio they can have their own container. Since children always want to experience things using all their senses, it is best to choose plants that grow quickly, look colourful and are also robust. Marigolds and zinnias fulfil these requirements. Children can pick a bunch of them and it will not matter, for more flowers will soon be produced. To appeal to a child's sense of smell, you should not forget to plant sweet peas and four o'clock flowers in the boxes. For a shady wigwam you need an orange box full of compost. Stick a long wooden pole into each corner and tie the poles together at the top. Now you can plant rapid-growing summer climbers, for example scarlet runner beans, at the base of each pole, and after a few weeks the sides of the tent will be almost covered.

For somewhat older children, you can plant a few cherry tomato plants in the boxes. These tomatoes taste particularly sweet. Of course, children love eating strawberries, and these will do well anywhere. Depending on the variety, you can train strawberry plants up trellises or you can let them dangle their fruit over the edge of a box or hanging basket. Nature also has something to offer impatient children. Cress and radishes are excellent for experimenting with nature.

*A real 'flower mum' makes sure that her children have enough to drink. The* Brachycome multifida, *however, soon reacts badly to too much care and attention, for excess water drowns its roots, causing the leaves to turn yellow.*

Just two days after sowing, the first green shoots appear. A few days later the cress, which is rich in vitamin C, can be eaten with bread and butter. A pumpkin plant is also fun. It is easy to grow if planted in a large tub. In the autumn, you can then hollow out the pumpkin to make a face for Hallowe'en. A banana plant is ideal for children. Every few days a new leaf unfurls. Do not take any risks when buying plants for a children's container, and be sure only to choose plants that are not poisonous.

## Suitable plants for children

All herbs and spices
**Vegetables:** radishes, lettuce and cress
**Summer flowers:** *Tagetes*, Surfinia petunias, *Zinnia*, *Scaevola*.
**For growing from seed:** nasturtiums, *Papaver*, *Tropaeolum*, wild flower mixtures, sunflower, *Convolvulus tricolor*.
**Scented plants:** *Lathyrus odoratus*, *Reseda*, *Mirabilis*.

*This setting makes you want to join in and play at the water tub. Half the playroom has been moved outdoors. With so much fresh air, the children's cheeks soon turn pink. The kiwi 'Jenny' will only bear fruit next year, since this year it has not come into flower.*

147

# Nature conservation: wild plants

If you want to find out more about nature through your patio or balcony, the many species of wild flowers will fit the bill. In choosing such plants, you will be bringing unadulterated nature on to your display which will not be one of magnificent, overflowing blooms. Instead, you will be rewarded by the sweet, simple charm of individual blooms that fill you with wonder when you take a closer look at them. A setting decorated with plants that nature produces of its own accord is one on which to make discoveries.

Among the native wild flowers are the summer flowers that you can usually sow straight from the seed packet. These only have one peak flowering period and do not offer non-stop blooms from spring to late autumn as is required of the typical cultivated forms of container flowers. Their charm is revealed if you watch them develop and modestly unfold their generally delicate, single blooms. Among the plants with an individual wild character are the corn cockle, toadflax, rose of heaven and corn poppy.

These wild flowers do not require you to put in the amount of work that is necessary for other summer blooms, so you can go ahead and turn your display into an ecological niche with many delightful wild plants. People feel attracted by such a place, and so do bumble bees, bees, hover flies, butterflies, ladybirds and, last but not least, birds. Many of these simple but beautiful flowers are scented and have attractive foliage. Examples are *Reseda, Matthiola, Mirabilis* and other scented plants. In nature, many of these attractive wild flowers grow on barren heathland, stony ground or rubbish tips. This means that they do not need nutrient-rich compost, preferring light, sandy soils low in nutrients. You do not need to use expensive peat and only a small amount of fertilizer will be necessary. The most environmentally friendly mixture is one made from bark humus and sand.

*A collection of meadow wild flowers such as in this container provides a real treat for the senses. This colourful mixture was planned well in advance; the individual summer flowers were sown in March on the windowsill and later planted at random in the box. Larkspur, African daisy, mallow, godetia, everlasting flower, rose of heaven, Cosmos sulphureus, mignonette and sage all require compost with a low nutrient content and need relatively little feeding and watering.*

*Papaver rhoeas* (corn poppy), *Phacelia, Agrostemma githago* (corn cockle), *Centaurea cyanus* (cornflower), *Chrysanthemum, Sinapis.*

The plants in this shell amphora are growing wild and untamed. Wild flowers spring up out of all the pockets. The Alstroemeria has many-coloured blooms on stems that grow to quite a height but nevertheless resist even strong winds successfully. Wild marjoram with its long stems is equally wind-resistant and attracts masses of butterflies. The evening primrose has found its way out of the shell-shaped pockets and up to the light. In the evenings it imparts its delightful scent that attracts moths. The Sedum or stonecrop has already been living in its pocket for a few years and now reaches down to the ground. All the wild flowers are either sown directly into the amphora or have been patiently sitting in their places for several years, withdrawing into the pockets during the winter.

**SITUATION:** sunny.
**COMPOST:** John Innes No. 1 or equivalent.
**CARE:** undemanding. For this plant to develop masses of flowers, it needs well-drained compost that is low in lime.
**PROPAGATION:** sowing the seed on a windowsill is child's play and is always successful.

*The everlasting flower has blooms that could be made of tissue paper (left).*

*The corn cockle flowers from July onwards (below).*

## *Agrostemma githago*

(Corn cockle)

This very dainty caryophyllaceous plant has lovely gleaming pink flowers with white centres. In the wild, it grows in corn fields and on rubbish tips, and it likes to have its roots in poor soil even in a container. This wild beauty blooms from June to July and is a real collector's plant.
**SITUATION:** sunny.
**COMPOST:** John Innes No. 1.
**CARE:** undemanding.
**PROPAGATION:** by seed sown directly where it is to grow.

## *Helipterum roseum*

(Everlasting flower)

This delightful flower produces blooms in white, golden yellow, pink and red and is suitable for cutting and drying. The blooms look as if they were made from tissue paper and rustle just like it if you brush against them. If you want to use them to make an arrangement, you will have to take the whole plant out of the box before it reaches the peak of its flowering period and hang it upside down in a shady, airy place out of the rain. Arrangements made from these flowers keep for many months and will remind you of a beautiful summer on the patio or balcony.

Cosmos sulphureus *in yellow and orange.*

## Cosmos sulphureus

*Cosmos sulphureus* with its brilliant semi-double blooms in strong shades of orange is a real straggler that only begins flowering at the end of July. It gets going when other flowers such as the corn cockle and corn poppy are already dying down. The stems with their feathery foliage tend to grow out sideways, but *Cosmos* produces pretty flowers tirelessly. Shades of orange are generally rather difficult to combine with other colours – white and blue are your best bet. The cornflower with its strong blue colour therefore makes an ideal companion.
**SITUATION:** sunny.
**COMPOST:** John Innes No. 2.
**CARE:** undemanding.
**PROPAGATION:** in March/April by seed on the windowsill.

## Papaver rhoeas

(Corn poppy)

This plant used to grow freely in our fields where it made itself very unpopular with farmers. However, it is once again in favour and can be seen opening its buds and unfurling its pretty flowers beside many country roads. It is one of the best-loved 'weeds' and no lover of wildflowers would be without it. It is fascinating to watch its hairy stems emerge and grow. This fiery, wild summer beauty can be sown directly where it is to grow. Poppies are now available with double blooms and in many reddish pastel shades.
**SITUATION:** sunny.
**COMPOST:** well-drained, John Innes No. 2 or equivalent.
**CARE:** undemanding.
**PROPAGATION:** sow the seeds directly where it is to grow.

*The corn poppy is available in many shades of red.*

*The dainty rose of heaven.*

## Silene coeli-rosa

(Rose of heaven)

Wild flower fans will be delighted with this dainty plant. The *Silene* is often confused with the single pink because of the similarity of its flowers and leaves. An annual, the rose of heaven is a native of the Mediterranean where it grows to about 80 cm (31 inches) in height. There are low-growing varieties suitable for growing in containers that are often listed under the name *Viscaria* in seed catalogues. The cultivar 'Blauer Engel' has sky-blue flowers and 'Rose Angel' has brilliant carmine blooms. Both varieties have a dark centre and flower from June to August.
**SITUATION:** full sun.
**COMPOST:** John Innes No. 2 or equivalent.
**CARE:** this plant does not like being waterlogged and must be tidied up occasionally.
**PROPAGATION:** by seed on the windowsill.

## Nigella damascena

(Love-in-a-mist)

This nice summer flower with needle-like leaves holds two attractions. In June it has pretty light-blue and white flowers that give way to decorative seed pods suitable for cutting and drying. When all the seed capsules have been formed, the plant is cut down and hung upside down to dry in a shady, airy place.
This delicate summer flower is often used to fill in the gaps in summer groups and taken out again once it has finished flowering. It grows to about 50-60 cm (20-24 inches) high in a pot.
Situation: sunny.
**COMPOST:** well-drained, John Innes No. 2.
**CARE:** undemanding.
**PROPAGATION:** by seed sown directly in the box.

Nigella: *the seed pods are also popular when dried.*

*The cornflower is simple to grow from seed.*

## Centaurea cyanus

(Cornflower)

Together with the corn poppy, the cornflower is one of the most popular wild flowers that used to grow in fields. However, the native blue cornflower has almost completely disappeared from our fields and is now making a comeback on patios or balconies where wild flowers are grown. The cornflower is available in white, pink and light-blue with double flowers. It can be sown directly in the box until May and flowers from June through to October. When on its own in a pot, it does splendidly and grows to 60 cm (24 inches) high.
**SITUATION:** sun to semi-shade.
**COMPOST:** John Innes No. 1.
**CARE:** undemanding.
**PROPAGATION:** sow from April directly in the box.

# Evergreen the whole year: the all-season display

If you do not have much time for gardening, you should resort to the easy-to-maintain all-season display. Once tubs, boxes, compost and plants are in place, they only need a minimum of care and attention, yet they provide you with a green setting all year round.

An all-season display does not give you non-stop blooms from spring to autumn, for you cannot expect hardy herbaceous perennials and woody plants, many of them native species, to come up with the display of blooms that subtropical plants can provide.

However, this is not what an all-season display is about, for its attraction lies in the natural charm of the plants.

*Sunshine bathes the fresh spring greenery of the conifers and woody plants in warm light, and the wooden bench promises many peaceful and contemplative hours. Yew, maple and box have grown to make a little wood. The rich variety of shapes alone that these trees offer gives you plenty to look at. Ceramic balls and pansies provide an additional homely touch.*

155

*A small spring garden at a lofty height. Miniature woody plants grow in a home-made balcony box between clump-forming spring herbaceous perennnials and tulips. Once planted, this balcony box will come into flower every spring, each time a little more luxuriantly.*

*Armeria maritima* (sea pink), *Aubrieta x cultorum* (aubrietia hybrid), *Pinus strobus* 'Minima' (pine), *Juniperus horizontalis* 'Glauca' (juniper), *Hedera helix* (ivy), *Phlox subulata* (phlox), *Abies koreana* 'Brevifolia' (Korean fir), *Prunus x cistena* (purple-leaf sand cherry), *Phlox* 'Chattahoochee' (phlox), *Pinus mugo* 'Humpy' (miniature dwarf pine).

important to get the proportions of woody plants and herbaceous perennials correct. The size of the diaplay should also be taken into account so that the plants do not grow too large for the space available. Before buying, you must be certain to find out about the growth habits and flowering periods of your long-term container guests. The following design suggestions should only serve as inspiration and can be infinitely elaborated upon. Conifers, woody plants and herbaceous perennials are particularly recommended as they are all hardy. However, even plants that are known to withstand frost

The trees and shrubs bring a piece of nature on to your patio or balcony, enabling you to watch the changes that the seasons bring at close quarters. Most hardy herbaceous perennials and woody plants gear their biological rhythm to their peak flowering period in spring, summer or autumn. Choose plants that as far as possible look good at all times of the year. Even a small area will then give you the opportunity to experience the natural cycles undisturbed and at close quarters.

All-season plantings look best if you take nature as your model. Use woody plants to give a basic structure to your design. These are then complemented by herbaceous perennials, grasses and bulbs. They all go well together and heighten each other's effect if their flowers or leaves develop at the same time. It is vitally

*Dwarf woody plants and small-flowered wild herbaceous perennials go well together and complement one another excellently. Since the woody plants almost all require compost with a low nutrient content, flowers with similar requirements should be chosen to go with them.*

*Penstemon barbatus* (beardtongue), *Glechoma hederacea* 'Variegata' (ground ivy), *Picea abies* 'Little Gem' (dwarf common spruce), *Cotoneaster horizontalis* (wall-spray), *Campanula carpatica* (bellflower), *Juniperus communis* 'Gold Cone' (dwarf common juniper).

must, **without fail,** be provided with insulation for their root balls, because the roots reach right out to the walls of the pot and are therefore directly exposed to frost *(see practical advice section).*

**For the small display** only the true dwarf and miniature woody plants can be considered. These are plants that grow very slowly under natural conditions and therefore require only a small amount of living space for years on end. Do not be tempted into buying a 'small' conifer without knowing what size it will be when fully grown. There are special 'Lilliputian' varieties for containers that can never reach tree size. These natural dwarfs grow decidedly slowly and can remain for a long time in the same container without having to be pruned regularly. The plant's identity and growth habit can only be deduced from a label that gives the exact name and variety. For this reason, when buying plants, go to specialist tree nurseries. That way you will get exactly what you want. Do not be deterred by the high price of true dwarf and miniature woody plants. It is in the very nature of these slow-growing trees and shrubs that cultivation takes a long time, making them more expensive.

### Designing a setting that is close to nature with dwarf woody plants and herbaceous perennials

The evergreen dwarf woody plants

will fire your enthusiasm with their many and varied forms. You can draw up a very exciting basic design for your containers using them. Columns and standards stretch upwards, while bushy or ball-shaped dwarf woody plants form a transition between them and woody plants of creeping habit. Nature is rarely symmetrical, so you should avoid planting little trees the same distance apart. Even 'monocultures' do not occur in nature, so the effect is more attractive if the entire box is not planted monotonously with conifers.

To make a 'mixed forest' in your container, plant slow-growing deciduous trees among the conifers. These will change their appearance with the seasons and create an attractive contrast to the evergreen conifers. Any gaps can then be filled with clump-forming alpines, grasses and bulbs. If you particularly love the spring or go away on holiday in summer, clump-forming herbaceous perennials that bloom in spring will be ideal as interplanting.

For summer, there is a long list of herbaceous perennials that flower for many weeks at a time. Small-flowering wild herbaceous perennials are most suitable for combining with dwarf woody plants since they are in proportion with them. Conifers all require a small amount of nutrients and can only be combined with plants with similar requirements. Since most summer flowers are dependent

### Specimen woody plants and showpiece herbaceous perennials for large areas

Vigorous-growing woody plants and tall showpiece herbaceous perennials are best planted in large tubs or containers placed on the floor. In the overall design of the display, the main features consist of small-crowned dwarf trees that are full of character. They look particularly attractive in the company of shrubs (e.g. *Spiraea bumalda*), conifers (e.g. *Pinus montana*), showpiece herbaceous perennials (e.g. *Rudbeckia*) and grasses (e.g. *Pennisetum)*. Shrubs that have long, spreading branches such as lilac are not suitable even for large settings. To provide privacy, you can grow perennial woody climbers (page 172) or tall shrubs with soft foliage such as bamboo. Unoccupied planting areas in the tubs and containers can then be filled with ground-cover plants.

### Hardiness of woody plants

Woody plants and herbaceous perennials that are overwintered in containers are subjected to particularly harsh conditions because the root balls are exposed to frost on all sides. Fine roots are the parts of a plant that are most susceptible to frost. Individual species differ widely in how frost-tender their roots are. While robust woody plants (*Pinus* and *Juniperus* varieties as well as *Thujopsis*) will tolerate temperatures down to -18°C (0° F), more sensitive plants such as *Ilex* and *Taxus* quickly fall victim to frost at below -10°C (14° F). In areas where the climate is harsh and there are persistent frosts, and especially in boxes hung on the outside of the railings, unprotected root balls soon freeze right through. However, if plants are placed on the floor up against the house wall, they receive protection from two sides.

*Sweetbriar*

**Macroclimate:** If you live in an area with a harsh climate, it is advisable to limit yourself to robust woody plants, at least for the basic design.

**Microclimate:** The microclimate on a patio or balcony is influenced by many factors and can vary to a greater or lesser degree from the regional climate. Situations in urban areas, on hillsides and close to walls are all favourable as regards climatic conditions.

**Problem situations: east- and south-facing situations:**
Evergreen plants in particular are at risk in these settings in the winter when the morning and midday sun shines on unprotected plants after frosty nights. Evergreen foliage plants in particular are rapidly damaged by the drastic thawing process while the soil is still frozen. In addition, east winds quickly lead to the dreaded drying-out of leaves or needles in winter. Evergreens that will also tolerate east- and south-facing situations are *Pinus* and *Juniperus* varieties.

### Woody plants that remain small

**Full sun:**
BROAD-LEAVED WOODY PLANTS:
*Caryopteris* (bluebeard)
*Cotoneaster* (creeping varieties) (dwarf medlar)
*Cytisus decumbens* (broom)
*Daphne cneorum* (daphne, poisonous!)
*Erica carnea* (winter-flowering heather)
*Potentilla* (five-finger, low-growing varieties)
*Genista lydia* (Bulgarian broom)
CONIFERS:
*Juniperus communis* 'Compressa' (dwarf, erect common juniper)
*Juniperus communis* 'Repanda' (prostrate, creeping common juniper)

*Juniperus communis* 'Siberica' (blue, dwarf common juniper)
*Juniperus horizontalis* 'Glauca' (blue, creeping juniper)
*Juniperus squamata* 'Blue Carpet' (blue, prostrate flaky juniper)
*Pinus mugo* 'Mops' (rounded dwarf pine)
*Pinus pumila* 'Glauca' (blue, dwarf Siberian pine)
*Pinus strobus* 'Radiata' (Monterey pine)

**Semi-shade:**
DECIDUOUS WOODY PLANTS:
*Calluna vulgaris* (ling, Scotch heather)
*Betula nana* (dwarf birch)
*Berberis buxifolia* 'Nana' (green, arching barberry)
*Euonymus fortunei* cultivars (spindle tree)
*Prunus x cistena*
*Salix purpurea* 'Nana' (purple osier)
*Rhododendron yakushimanum* and *R. repens* (rhododendron)
CONIFERS:
*Abies balsamea* 'Nana' (dwarf Balsam fir)
*Abies koreana* 'Brevifolia' (dwarf Korean fir)
*Chamaecyparis lawsoniana* 'Minima Glauca' (blue, dwarf, globular Lawson cypress)
*Chamaecyparis obtusa* 'Nana Gracilis' (small Hinoki cypress)
*Chamaecyparis pisifera* 'Boulevard' (small Sawara cypress)
*Microbiota decussata* (Komar)
*Picea abies* 'Echiniformis' (Norway spruce)
*Picea glauca* 'Conica' (white spruce)
*Picea omorika* 'Nana' (dwarf Serbian spruce)
*Thuja orientalis* 'Aurea Nana' (the most attractive rounded dwarf form of Chinese thuja with yellow needles)

*Tsuga canadensis* 'Nana' (dwarf Canada hemlock)

**Shade:**
DECIDUOUS WOODY PLANTS:
*Buxus sempervirens* 'Suffruticosa' (box)
*Pieris japonica* (lily-of-the-valley bush)
*Skimmia japonica*
*Vinca minor* (lesser periwinkle)
CONIFERS:
*Thujopsis dolabrata* (hiba)
*Taxus baccata*, low-growing varieties (only hardy with good root ball insulation)

## Specimen woody plants for containers

**Full sun:**
DECIDUOUS WOODY PLANTS:
*Betula* (birch)
*Choenomeles speciosa* (ornamental quince)
*Rhus typhina* (stag's-horn sumach)
CONIFERS:
*Juniperus communis* 'Hibernica' (common juniper)
*Juniperus virginiana* 'Skyrocket' (pencil cedar)
*Pinus cembra* (Arolla pine)

**Semi-shade:**
DECIDUOUS WOODY PLANTS:
*Acer palmatum* (Japanese maple)
*Euonymus* (spindle tree)
*Sinarundinaria* (bamboo)
CONIFERS:
*Chamaecyparis lawsoniana* varieties (Lawson cypress)
*Picea orientalis* 'Aurea' (Oriental spruce)
*Thuja occidentalis* varieties (American arbor vitae)

**Shade:**
DECIDUOUS WOODY PLANTS:
*Ilex aquifolium* (common holly)
*Laburnum* (laburnum)
*Hamamelis virginiana* (Virginian witchhazel)
CONIFERS:
*Taxus baccata* (yew, insulate root ball!)
*Taxus media* 'Hicksii'
*Tsuga canadensis* (Canada hemlock)

**Herbaceous perennials, grasses and bulbs:**
The enchanting world of herbaceous perennials, grasses and bulbs is also available to the owner of an all-season display, for most of these plants thrive between trees and shrubs in boxes and containers.

*Ornamental quince.*

# A luxuriant start to spring

*In this spring box of scented plants, dwarf columbine, saxifrage and forget-me-not are grouped around a small apple tree.*

*Malus* **'Golden Hornet'** (ornamental apple), *Aquilegia flabellata* **'Ministar'** (columbine), *Myosotis sylvatica* (forget-me-not), *Saxifraga-Arendsii* hybrids (saxifrage), *Hedera helix* (common ivy).

This romantic setting is not just an all-season one, for the boxes are kept free for seasonal planting. The woody plants form a green framework around seasonal flowers that are planted in the boxes as the mood takes you. Biennials such as forget-me-nots, daisies and violets make a particularly attractive accompaniment to spring-flowering woody plants. They were planted in the boxes in autumn, grouped together in a sheltered place and wrapped up for the winter. Only the daisies were purchased from the garden centre in the spring. By autumn, the Japanese ornamental quince will have produced its very decorative fruits.

**Tulipa** hybrids (tulips), **Bellis perennis** (double daisies), **Chaenomeles speciosa** (ornamental quince), **Clematis alpina** (clematis), **Lonicera caprifolia** (honeysuckle), **Rhododendron yakushimanum** (rhododendron), **Aquilegia flabellata** 'Ministar' (columbine), **Myosotis sylvatica** (forget-me-not).

In April, the catkins and early spring flowers make an eye-catching display. The standard weeping willow is grafted on to a slow-growing creeping willow. This robust tree can therefore remain in the same container for a long time.

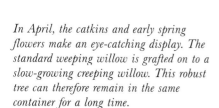

**Salix repens** 'Jona' (grafted on to creeping willow), **Crocus vernus** (crocus), **Scilla siberica** 'Alba' (Siberian squill).

# Summer brings greenery and flowers

A very robust group has been planted in this box in a sunny to semi-shaded situation. The potentilla is a typical summer-flowering shrub. Each flower lasts for two weeks, and they continue to be produced into autumn. The yellow leaves of the Euonymus emphasize the brilliance of the potentilla blooms. Even the Iceland poppy with its yellow and orange flowers blends well with this colour scheme and blooms without a break from June to September. The hiba is a model of resilience, for any situation from sun to shade suits it. The sedge with its fine, reddish-brown fronds provides variety of texture in this group of plants. Conifers like evenly moist soil, so you should not forget to water them.

Potentilla 'Kobold' (potentilla), *Carex buchananii* (sedge), *Euonymus* 'Emerald's Gold' (spindle), *Papaver nudicaule* (Iceland poppy), *Hedera helix* (common ivy), *Thujopsis dolabrata* (hiba).

Even in a shady situation you can make yourself a space surrounded by greenery using trees and shrubs. As long as the setting does not lie in deep shadow and open sky still shows above it, many woody plants that in the wild make up the undergrowth in a wood will feel at home there. Valuable Japanese maple varieties have been chosen as the centre-piece on this display: these woody plants, that are grown for their foliage, begin to produce their beautiful shoots in early spring. From these emerge the extremely decorative laciniate leaves that range from light green to dark red in colour. The full-moon maple has reddish-purple flowers that appear in mid-spring, but the tree's beauty peaks in autumn when its leaves change colour to fiery shades of yellow, orange and red. The slow-growing trees will not grow any higher than 3 metres (10 feet) in their containers. In their native Japan they like growing near water, so they appreciate the refreshing humidity that rises from the container of water. A bamboo affords a good degree of privacy and, since it also keeps its pale green leaves in winter, there will be something green to look at during the gloomy months of the year. In May, the little deutzia is covered in scores of white flowers. Between the woody plants are various herbaceous perennials grown for their foliage or flowers that are particularly suited to life near water.

*Deutzia gracilis, Hosta sieboldiana* (plantain lily), *Sinarundinaria murielae* (syn. *Thamnocalamus*) (Muriel bamboo), *Acer palmatum* (Japanese maple), *Acer japonicum* 'Aconitifolium' (full-moon maple), *Acer palmatum* 'Atropurpureum' (red-leaved Japanese maple), *Alchemilla mollis* (lady's mantle), *Iris pseudocorus* (yellow flag), *Iris sibirica* (Siberian flag).

*The compact and extremely free-flowering azaleas of the Diamant group are particularly well suited to planting in boxes. The semi-evergreen azaleas are available in many bright colours. They have proved to be amazingly hardy, but you should not take any risks with these little treasures and give them good protection for the winter.*

**Azaleas, Diamant group (rosy-red), 'Palestrina', 'Kirin'.**

*As long as the setting is not in deep shade, evergreens make ideal subjects for the shady patio or balcony. To provide variety and colour for the boxes in summer, you could plant shade-tolerant summer flowers. Fuchsias and begonias will not be so luxuriant because of the low concentration of fertilizer used for the other plants, but they will manage some flowers. Sink a roomy outer pot down in between the woody plants so that you can add and remove potted seasonal plants quickly without damaging the roots of the long-term residents.*

*Buxus sempervirens* **'Suffruticosa'**, *Buxus sempervirens* **'Herrenhausen'** (box), *Begonia semperflorens* (begonia), *Fuchsia* hybrids (fuchsia), *Hedera helix* (common ivy).

A decorative little box for a display in full sun. Grey-leaved scented plants and kitchen herbs fit harmoniously into the combination of useful and ornamental plants. As natives of the south, they love full sun but are otherwise very modest in their requirements. The box is only 60 cm (24 inches) long but is so cleverly planted that it does not look ostentatious yet nevertheless conceals many surprises. The Cheddar pink hangs down over the edge of the box and blooms from May until well into June. Then it is the turn of the lavender with its delicate blue flowers. The marjoram is in flower from June and attracts many butterflies. In between, the lily opens its luxuriant blooms and draws people's gaze. The thyme with its incomparable fragrance is almost lost among the other plants. Right at the back is sage, whose leaves can be harvested to make a herb tea. The delicate grass mingles playfully with its neighbours and lends a lively note to the entire planting. The wood sorrel has sneakily sown itself, but is allowed to stay. Finally, the Alpine thistle produces its silver-grey flower heads that remind one for some time to come of the colourful activity of summer.

*Lavandula angustifolia* **'Munstead'** **(lavender),** *Stipa* **(grass),** *Dianthus gratianopolitanus* **(Cheddar pink),** *Lilium* **hybrid 'Stargazer' (lily),** *Origanum vulgare* **(wild marjoram),** *Thymus x citriodorus* **'Variegatus' (thyme),** *Salvia officinalis* **(sage),** *Carlina acaulis* **(Alpine thistle).**

# The magic of roses in containers

Roses have been very popular for centuries and are currently conquering the patio or balcony. Rose enthusiasts who live in towns can now keep the queen of flowers very successfully in containers and boxes. There are dwarf varieties that will make do with large window boxes. They grow 30-40 cm (12-16 inches) high and bloom for many months in summer.

Taller-growing shrub roses are not suitable for small settings. They take up too much space and severely limit your freedom of movement. On the other hand, a standard rose does not take up much space at the level where you want to sit and will provide shade on a sunny day. The most beautiful and rewarding cultivar that can be found grown as a standard is 'Snow White', with its pleasantly scented white blooms.

Roses are sold in quite large pots and so need a container that is at least 20-30 cm (8-12 inches) wide and 30 cm (12 inches) high to accommodate the root ball. The queen of flowers does not like it either if the wind constantly tugs at her, so she needs a sheltered place. In contrast to other long-term guests, roses are quite demanding. They like quite a bit of care and attention. In the winter they either need a cool cellar, or should be well protected against frost. The following varieties are particularly suitable for the display: in spring the *Rosa chinensis* 'Minima' is available as a house plant. As a plant that needs light and fresh air, it feels much happier out of doors.

*Here successfully combined with bamboo, the standard roses, cultivar 'Iceberg', create an impression of simple elegance. 'Iceberg' is one of the most robust of roses and produces sweetly scented flowers without a break into autumn.*

*The semi-double, weather-resistant ground-cover rose 'Fair Play' is well suited to planting in a box. It has bright red blooms that fade to pink as they mature.*

The dwarf rose 'Sonnenkind' has double yellow blooms, while those of 'Baby Masquerade' are yellow-pink. The dense, cushion-forming dwarf bush rose 'The Fairy' and the bush rose 'Iceberg' do well in large containers.

**Ideal companions for roses** are bamboo (*Sinarundinaria*), box (*Buxus*), lavender (*Lavandula*), catmint (*Nepeta*), cotton lavender (*Santolina*) and grasses.

**COMPOST:** John Innes No. 2 or equivalent, roses like lime.

**CARE:** water regularly. Roses need a well-balanced fertilizer for healthy growth. They quickly react with chlorotic leaves to an excess of a particular nutrient or a lack of trace elements. The best plan is to scatter a slow-release fertilizer around the base of the plant once in spring and once in summer, depending on the type of fertilizer. In addition, give one application of a liquid micronutrient feed. It is very important that no more fertilizer should be given from August onwards. Roses impart their most powerful scent when planted in compost that contains only a moderate amount of nutrients and has a pH of more than 7. If you feed them too much it will be at the expense of their scent!

**OVERWINTERING:** hardy varieties can remain outdoors provided they are well wrapped up. Standards are best wrapped in straw matting. All parts of the plants that are above ground must either have straw matting or fir branches packed around them. This prevents the winter sunshine from drying them out. Frost-tender roses can be overwintered most successfully in a cellar, garage or shed. In spring, as the weather improves, the roses should be brought back into the open air so that they do not come into leaf too soon and grow rank.

**PRUNING:** dwarf roses are cut back to half their size before they come into leaf. Only the dead shoots are removed from standards.

**REPOTTING:** dwarf roses are repotted each year in fresh, nutrient-rich compost. In the case of larger roses, just the upper layer of compost is renewed in spring.

*The dwarf rose 'Sonnenkind'.*

# An autumnal close to the growing season

This is the spring box from page 160, now in its autumn colours. After the forget-me-nots had finished flowering, they were replaced by a low-growing balsam fir. Throughout the summer, the delicate Brachycome multifida *has enlived the* planting with its blue blooms. The autumnal high point is provided by the little apple tree. The numerous little red apples (for species see page 160) remain in place long into the winter until they are devoured by hungry birds.

Where would autumn be without golden grasses that sway in the breeze?
The warm evening sun bathes the barely 12-metre-square (130-feet-square) area in soft light. Grasses rock gently back and forth and, together with the first red-tinged leaves of the Virginia creeper, announce the approach of autumn. A Cotoneaster towers above the other plants.

*Cotoneaster x watereri* 'Pendulus' (cotoneaster), *Pennisetum compressum* (Chinese fountain grass), *Rudbeckia hirta* (coneflower), *Helianthus annuus* (sunflower), *Juniperus communis* 'Hibernica' (common juniper), *Chrysanthemum articum, Hordeum jubatum* (foxtail barley).

You can still enjoy the autumn display to the full. The ornamental grass rustles with every gentle breeze and its elegant fronds are bathed in the most beautiful warm light. The Virginia creeper is losing its foliage leaf by leaf. The container gardener is already thinking about spring, for now is the time to bury bulbs in the window box.

*Miscanthus floridulus* (ornamental grass), *Miscanthus sinensis* 'Variegatus' (ornamental grass), *Cotoneaster dammeri* 'Skogholm' (cotoneaster), *Chrysanthemum indicum* hybrids, *Pennisetum compressum* (Chinese fountain grass), peach tree with Virginia creeper.

# Nature has a rest

There is a festive mood: the 'feasting' has already begun for the birds because this Christmas tree is for them. Colourful apples and bags of nuts cheer the hearts of your feathered friends. Now that there is little food for them to find, a 'banquet' such as this is always welcome. As Christmas draws nearer, the tree will be stripped and brought indoors for a short while. Then the apples will be exchanged for glass baubles and the bags of nuts for chocolates. Fairy lights will bring a festive glow to the branches. It is important that you should not forget to water the tree while it is indoors. Even so, a living Christmas tree cannot remain indoors all the time until Twelfth Night because it will need fresh air. In spring, the fir tree will then delight you with its new light-green growth at the tips of its branches, while the birds will be able to fend for themselves again.

*Now all is white, still and festive. When the evergreen trees and shrubs are coated in snow, they have the best protection against drying out in the winter sunshine. If there is no snow, less hardy subjects should be covered with fibre fleece. Incidentally, not only the plants, but also the wood of the steamer chair will withstand frost.*

# *Perennial climbing plants*

Since a patio or balcony is generally very limited in size, you should remember to use the space in the vertical plane as well and incorporate it into your design. If you clothe the walls in a thick covering of perennial climbing plants, a quiet spot amid greenery will become reality. The leaves of the climbing plants filter the sunlight, generating a tranquil atmosphere. If the entire area is surrounded by a green forest of leaves, they will even trap the dust out of the air and make it more pleasant to breathe. A setting such as this can be a veritable ecological niche, offering many insects and small creatures a safe home. Naturally, hardy climbing plants take up more space than the annual species, but they can remain in place for many years, and each spring they start climbing again where they left off the previous autumn.

A sufficiently large container is needed to ensure healthy growth. Slower-growing climbers need at least a 30-litre (8-gallon) container and vigorous growers need a 50-litre (13-gallon) one. When planting, proceed as described on page 186.

*Tasty grapes hang from a vine.*

*Scented plants make this late spring setting an enchanting place. The container plants have now awoken from their winter sleep and contribute to the potpourri of scents until well into summer.*

> *Lonicera caprifolium* (**honeysuckle**), *Cytisus* (**broom**), *Pelargonium graveolens* (**scented geranium**), *Lavandula* (**lavender**), *Convallaria majalis* (**lily-of-the-valley**).

## *Vitis vinifera*

(Grape vine)

Even a grape vine can be grown successfully in a container. Wine lovers in particular will be enthusiastic about this ancient cultivated plant that has much to offer: beautiful vine leaves, fruit and a Bordeaux-red tint to its foliage in autumn. It requires a trellis to which its branches can

173

be attached and a deep tub with at least a 50-litre (13-gallon) capacity. A highly recommended cultivar which is resistant to disease is 'Boskoops Glory'.

**SITUATION:** sunny.

**COMPOST:** see practical advice section, the addition of loam is beneficial.

**CARE AND OVERWINTERING:** see practical advice section.

## *Parthenocissus* hybrids

(Virginia creeper)

When planted in a garden against a house wall, a Virginia creeper can cover a several-storeyed house in a green mantle within a few years. It is a vigorous climber that wants to go ever upwards. In summer, it has attractive leaves that are strong green in colour, turning to a wonderful, relaxing red in autumn. The Virginia creeper definitely needs a large

Clematis macropetala

tub so that it can spread out its roots. *Parthenocissus quinquefolia* (Virginia creeper) has five-lobed leaves and needs a trellis up which to climb. *P. tricuspidata* (Boston ivy) has three-lobed leaves and adheres straight to the wall of its own accord. When it has covered all the wall, its shoots hang downwards to form a green curtain. Both creepers turn a wonderful carmine red in autumn.

**SITUATION:** sunny to semi-shade.

**COMPOST:** standard compost.

**CARE:** feed every 6-8 weeks.

**OVERWINTERING:** the tubs need to be insulated, then the plants can

Parthenocissus *hybrid in autumn*

be overwintered outdoors. Frost-damaged shoots are cut back in spring when new growth will appear at the base.

## *Clematis* hybrids

(Clematis)

As a patio or balcony owner, you need not be without these beautiful climbing plants with their charming star-shaped blooms. Particularly suitable are the slow-growing and early-flowering varieties such as *Clematis alpina* and *C. macropetala*. The cultivars 'Nelly Moser' and 'The President' are especially pretty and to be recommended. The buds are formed in the previous year on the tips of the branches and open in May during the main flowering period. In September, there follows a second flowering on the new shoots. A clematis will climb to a height of several metres (10 feet or more) and will need some kind of support. If your clematis is getting out of hand, you can easily check its growth by cutting it back. In any case, it should be cut right back every 2-3 years. A clematis likes to have its roots in moist compost in the shade. The best plan is to put a ground-cover plant in the same container with it, or to cover the compost with a mulch of bark chippings or pebbles.

**SITUATION:** this plant likes to grow in the dappled shade of trees and prefers a place in semi-shade.

**PLANTING:** the tub should be at least 50 cm (20 inches) in diameter and 40 cm (16 inches) deep. Provide drainage so that waterlogging cannot occur.

**COMPOST:** the clematis will remain for several years in the same compost, so it must be light, airy and well-draining. Enough long-acting fertilizer for a year should be mixed in with the compost before planting.

**CARE:** be sure to keep the compost evenly damp.

**DISEASES:** the early-flowering varieties have the advantage that they are not susceptible to clematis wilt.

## *Aristolochia macrophylla*

(Dutchman's pipe)

A native of America, this twining plant climbs ever upwards, unfurling its pretty, soft leaves that can be as much as 30 cm (12 inches) across and are bright green in spring.

The flowers are barely visible among the foliage, are purple in

*The luxuriant green of Dutchman's pipe.*

colour and shaped like long-stemmed pipes. The plant can grow many metres (feet) high if given a suitably large pot, and its large leaves afford plenty of privacy.

**SITUATION:** semi-shade to shade.

**COMPOST:** standard compost, well-drained, but kept moist.

**CARE:** water regularly, must not be allowed to dry out. Feed once a month.

**OVERWINTERING:** provide root ball insulation.

## *Hedera* hybrids

(Ivy)

With these vigorous green climbing plants you will bring colour and a snug atmosphere to a shady north-facing setting. Grey façade walls will be covered with a cosy carpet of green. Ivy has the advantage that it retains its leaves in winter, giving you something green to look at all year round. You do not need a trellis for ivy, because it will climb up a wall by

*Ivy loves shade.*

itself using its adventitious rootlets. It remains unaffected by wind and weather, and it even withstands polluted city air. If you want to brighten up your display, do not choose an ivy with dark green leaves, but buy a variegated one that has white, silvery grey or yellow markings, or one that has light green leaves. If it is to survive the winter, the ivy should be planted in its tub in spring.

A suitable cultivar for containers is the yellow to lime-green 'Goldcraft'. If the ivy refuses to climb up a wall, it could either be the nature of your wall or the lighting conditions that are at fault. It does not like attaching its adventitious rootlets to walls with a high chalk content, and it does not like the sun shining directly on its leaves. If too much direct light strikes it or a white wall reflects bright sunlight on to it, it will grow away from the light.

**SITUATION:** semi-shade to shade.

**COMPOST:** loose, well-drained compost.

**CARE:** regular feeding from May to the end of August is required. Every 2-3 years the ivy should be repotted in spring and the shoots cut back a little.

# How to be a successful container gardener

You do not have to be a gardener to put the planting ideas we have suggested into practice. Even beginners will achieve rapid success if they keep to the most important basic rules for looking after plants. The first step is to make the right choice of plants, according to the criteria laid down in this book – taking into account lighting conditions, nutrient requirements, and so on. Make a sketch of your planting scheme and buy the plants as soon as possible after mid-May. Make sure that you choose top-quality plants and do not try to cut corners by buying cheap compost. Settle the plants in their containers as soon as possible and do not forget to water them thoroughly. You must also remember to feed them the appropriate number of weeks after planting. All these criteria – described on the following pages – are vitally important if the plants are to do well.

If looked after with loving care according to their individual requirements, container plants will reward you with a luxuriant and long-lasting display of flowers.

*It is the start of summer. Containers and boxes have been scrubbed clean, and the watering can stands ready. Fresh compost and newly bought young plants await planting on the balcony.*

*From left to right: clay pot, plastic pot, peat pot and pot made from recycled paper. In front of the pots are plants that have been grown in cell seed trays.*

Only if you make basic mistakes when caring for plants, or are extremely unlucky with the weather, will they react by falling prey to pests and diseases on account of their weakened condition. We cannot influence the weather, but when plants languish and become sick under the best of conditions, this is mostly due to the wrong type of care. You need to learn to recognize the signs so that you can help the plants out of their predicament. Combating pests and diseases directly should always be seen as a last resort, and should only be carried out when the actual cause has been recognized and dealt with.

## What you should look for when buying plants

Each year, summer bedding plants seem to arrive earlier and earlier in garden centres. Do not be tempted to buy the tender young plants as early as April. It is difficult for the keen gardener to walk past this varied display, but the plants will have to be protected until mid-May if bought any earlier. If the plants have already been put in their boxes, you will have to expect frosts nightly. The delicate baby plants will then need a protective cover or a warm place to spend the night. The experienced gardener waits until after mid-May to go to the nursery and puts the young plants into their boxes straight away so that they can develop without danger of frost damage.

Container flowers are sold in different sizes and quantities. The simplest method involves growing young plants in polystyrene seed trays. They are propagated from cuttings or from seed, and are sold in their cells either in strips or rectangular trays. Young vegetables, too, can be sold in this way.

Since the young plants sold in polystyrene trays are seldom advanced enough to have flowers, it is often very difficult to decide on the best colour combination. Usually, however, the nurseryman will be able to tell you the colours. Container flowers sold in pots are somewhat more expensive. These are considerably larger plants that often have a good number of buds. With these you can identify the different colours immediately.

When buying, make sure that the plants have healthy green leaves. Check carefully to see whether they have enough strong buds. The plants should be compact in shape and should not have long, rank shoots, for such plants will never grow to a good shape.

The root ball must show plenty of roots and no pests should be visible under the leaves. Spots on the leaves indicate fungal infection. In the case of plants grown from bulbs, you should make sure that the bulbs are good and firm and that the skin is undamaged.

# Compost for seasonal planting

Apart from light and air, plants need water and nutrients to live, and these they absorb from the soil through their roots.

With seasonal planting, the compost must be changed completely every year, otherwise pathogens from the previous year could be present in the compost which would rapidly attack the new plants. Usually, by the end of the container season, the compost has been penetrated throughout by the roots of the summer flowers which will have completely exhausted it. If you are aiming for a luxuriant display of blooms every year, you should look for a good quality compost. If you try to make savings here, you will not be rewarded by a long-lasting display of flowers.

Our container flowers can be divided into three large groups according to their nutrient requirements:

*Successful combinations of plants:*
*Left: those with a moderate and high nutrient requirement;*
*Right: those with a moderate and low nutrient requirement.*

## Plants with a low nutrient requirement

This group includes most wild flowers and cultivated plants that retain their wild character, having been little altered by plant breeders and generally having small flowers and leaves. Examples are *Thynophylla, Brachycome, Nemesia* and *Linum.* Their natural growth habit is modest, and they like having their roots in thin, light soil that is low in nutrients, which is where they do best.

For these plants use John Innes No. 1 compost or an equivalent seedling compost, or mix 20% sand in with John Innes No. 2 compost.

## Plants with a moderate nutrient requirement

Most summer flowers belong to this group.

John Innes No. 2 compost or equivalent is best suited to this group.

## Plants with a high nutrient requirement

Summer flowers that have been given large blooms and continuous flowering ability as a result of plant breeding belong to this group. Examples are geraniums and *Petunia surfinia* hybrids. However, a few container plants such as oleander and *Canna* also belong to this group.

For these plants you need to use John Innes No. 3 compost, or give plenty of fertilizer subsequently if you use John Innes No. 2. If you do not give the plants this nourishment, they will stop blooming. For best results, combine plants that all have the same nutrient requirement.

Plants with a moderate nutrient requirement can also be combined with those with a low or high nutrient requirement. Additional fertilizer is then adapted to the needs of the partner that requires less. In this way, the more vigorous plants adapt to make a harmonious group with the more delicate ones. However, you should never combine flowers of a wild character with plants requiring a high nutrient content, as the former will fail to thrive because of the excess fertilizer, or the latter will hardly produce any blooms for lack of sufficient nutrients.

## The properties of compost

The best compost for all container flowers is light, airy and retentive of both water and nutrients.

Compost has the job of providing a secure hold for the plant and its branching root system.

# Soil as a reservoir of water and nutrients

The soil in which the plants are to thrive must possess the ability to bind nutrients that are added to it in order to make them available to the plants. **Clay and humus** carry out this task outstandingly well, with clay having a greater binding ability than humus. A high proportion of clay in the soil therefore protects the plants against 'overindulgence', i.e. against taking up too large a quantity of nutrients. This would cause them to produce luxuriant foliage at the expense of flowers, and plants with a low nutrient requirement would die.

The compost that you buy may already have had a large proportion of clay added to it by the manufacturer. Because of its binding ability, clay is able to intercept doses of fertilizer that are too large, thus protecting the plants from damage. Imprecise amounts of fertilizer, such as a beginner might easily administer, soon damage the plants if a compost based on peat alone is used.

However, the proportion of clay should not be too high either, for it makes the compost solid and has a detrimental effect on drainage.

Pure garden soil naturally has a high proportion of clay and is not suitable for container flowers in its pure form.

**Oxygen** is vitally necessary both for the plant's uptake of nutrients and for root growth.

Water and nutrients are absorbed by the plant's fine fibrous roots, which must be constantly renewed by continuous growth. Even when saturated with water, the compost must therefore still retain enough pores with air in them so that excess water can flow away at any time and the oxygen content of the soil be maintained. Waterlogging that persists for more than 6 hours causes the fine fibrous roots to rot and nutrients can no longer be absorbed. Finally, the **pH value** of the compost is of great importance. This is an indication of the acid content of the soil. The neutral pH value is 7.0, but most balcony flowers like a slightly acid soil with a pH of 5.5-6.5. At pH values that are too high or too low, various nutrients are no longer available to the plants, and signs of deficiency appear. If you always use hard tap water for watering, the pH value will rise and iron deficiencies will occur that cause the leaves to turn a chlorotic yellow. Tap water that is too soft will cause the pH to become increasingly acid. A high-quality compost has the ability to buffer the calcium carbonate so that the pH value remains constant.

# The different kinds of compost

**Peat:**
Modern peat-based growing mediums are the ones most frequently used because they do not weigh a great deal and they are also light in texture. However, the sphagnum bogs, which are important wildlife habitats, are destroyed by peat cutting because the peat does not 'grow' back. Many of the cheap composts sold as being suitable for containers and hanging baskets are purely peat-based. However, these are not as suitable for patio flowers since they do not contain any clay and are therefore not good at retaining nutrients.

Once it has dried out completely in the patio boxes, such compost is difficult to dampen again. If you try to water it, the water will simply run down the inside of the box and drip straight out of the drainage holes.

With a growing medium composed purely of peat, it is easy to administer too much fertilizer and signs of deficiency can soon occur. Of the peat-based composts, those that contain moisture- and nutrient-retaining substances are the most suitable.

There are composts for different purposes that are each adapted to the particular needs of the plants.

When peat is cut, two different qualities are obtained. One is a very fine peat and the other, of better quality, is coarser.

Coarse peat has the advantage that it holds much more air than fine peat. It has not decomposed to the extent of fine peat and because of this it has the ability to soak up six times its own volume of water. Even when fully saturated, it can still retain the 30% air content that is necessary for the roots to be able to breathe.

Unfortunately, at the time of writing this book, it has not yet become possible to do without peat entirely in the manufacture of compost for hanging basket and container use. Many institutes are busy carrying out research into the most suitable alternatives. The first stages have already been completed and a few products are already on the market. However, like all ecologically justifiable alternatives, they are somewhat more awkward to use and require more knowledge.

# Peat-free composts

There are some peat-free composts on the market such as ICI's Coir Multipurpose Compost or Fison's Levington Peat-free Universal Compost, but using them requires a certain amount of knowledge and skill to maintain the correct nutrient and moisture content.

### Garden compost

If you use large quantities of compost or make garden compost yourself, you can use garden compost in conjunction with loamy garden soil as a basis for your own home-made container compost. This is of course conditional upon the rotting process being complete, otherwise the introduction of such material could cause problems.

During the composting process you can add ingredients that contain clay such as loam. Mixed compost from kitchen rubbish is primarily composed of organic substances. These give the growing medium to which the compost is added a high pH and a low nitrogen content.

The big disadvantage of these types of compost is the high content of weed seeds that germinate in the containers and have to be constantly removed. Garden compost contains many micro-organisms, some of which have important parts to play. However, they also include fungi and bacteria that can cause seedlings and young plants to be subject to damping off.

Garden compost is therefore not suitable for propagation purposes unless you pack the soil mixture into roasting bags and sterilize it in the oven.

# How to plant correctly

If you have just returned from buying plants and do not have time to settle them straight away into their places, then put the young plants in the shade for the moment.

If you have bought plants that are not in pots, it is best to choose a cloudy day for planting them, or else wait until evening to do the job.

Young plants whose root balls have dried out should be placed in a tub of water for a while before planting so that they can become saturated with moisture.

Young plants that have just been planted up cannot tolerate hot sunshine immediately and should be shaded with fibre fleece or newspaper for a day. This makes it much easier for them to become established.

### Preparing containers

Check new containers for drainage holes. If there are none, you will have to drill some.

*From top to bottom:*
*covering the drainage holes, planting and watering in.*

*Avoid spraying the leaves when watering as this can encourage diseases.*

The containers must be carefully cleaned to remove all traces of the previous year's compost so that diseases will not be passed on to the new plants. Lay a crock or a stone across each drainage hole to prevent it from becoming blocked with compost. Since very few container plants will tolerate waterlogging, you should always provide a good drainage layer at the bottom of your boxes. You can use pebbles or pieces of broken flowerpot to form a layer 3-5 cm (1¹/₂-2 inches) deep.

Then fill the box with the right amount of compost to allow the root balls enough space and a 1-2 cm (¹/₂-³/₄ inch) gap between the surface of the compost and the top of the box. If the plants are not fully grown, they will need space around them in which to develop, so plant them the correct distance apart. Boxes that are only 10 cm (4 inches) wide can take just one row of plants, i.e. with the root balls placed in a line. Boxes that are 20 cm (9 inches) wide can take two rows. Arrange trailing plants in front with erect ones behind. Next, cover the root balls with compost, leaving a gap of at least 1 cm (¹/₂ inch) between the surface and the top of the box. Now firm the compost and root balls well with your fingers.

If you fill the box too full with compost, the water may overflow and run down the outside of the box, depriving the plants of their full share of moisture.

Finally, water everything thoroughly, and the plants will be all set to burst into prolific growth.

## How to water correctly

### When should you water?

Only water when the compost feels dry!

A drying-out period should always follow watering as the roots will rot if they remain in wet compost for too long.

Check the compost with your finger and only water if it feels dry but before the plants go limp. Remember that you will also need to water if there has been **rain** since raindrops mostly run off the leaves and over the side of the box.

### How should you water?

Preferably not too much at once, but keep going until the water drips out of the drainage holes. **Never** spray the leaves while watering as this encourages disease. Instead, position the neck of the watering can under the leaves so that the water falls directly onto the compost.

### How often should you water?

In the portrait section you will discover how much water a particular plant requires. In the cooler parts of the year during spring and autumn, watering once a day will be sufficient.

### Should you water in the morning or evening?

In spring and autumn you should water in the morning so that the plants can dry out again during the course of the day. In summer you should water both mornings and evenings.

The watering can should always be filled and placed in sunshine so that the water warms up before it is next needed. At the height of summer you will have to water several times during the day, and if the water is warm the plants will not receive a shock.

### Automatic watering

Watering is actually a pleasant task that gives you the chance to observe your plants and put the hectic day behind you. However, if you have long rows of plants to look after, watering can become a strenuous and time-consuming chore. This is where a watering system in which the flowers are planted in a box with a dual base comes in useful. The plants will then look after themselves for about two weeks, with the water being drawn up from the reservoir beneath the box by a length of capillary matting that acts as a wick.

The situation becomes more difficult if you want to go away in summer and do not trust anybody to look after your plants for you. You will then need to install an automatic watering system (such as the Gardena Micro-Drip-System). The savings that you make in terms of water and work will soon justify the cost of the necessary electrical and water installations. Do not be put off if the nearest water-pipes are far away from the patio. Flexible copper piping can be laid from the nearest water connection to your setting.

### Micro-drip watering

A micro-drip watering system consists of plastic piping, drip tubes and a humidity control system.

If you have access to both water and electricity connections, you can use an automatic watering system controlled by a tensiometer. Alternatively, some systems are battery-operated. A moisture sensor is pushed into the compost alongside the roots of a representative plant where it senses the changes in humidity and accordingly controls the water supply via an electrical regulator. A liquid fertilizer reservoir can also be connected into the system so that low doses of feed can be given with each watering. Such a system can lead to record-breaking displays of flowers with a minimum of work on your part. If you want to feed in rain water from a butt, this can also be done with a special purpose-designed pump. There are even tried-and-tested systems for situations without an electricity supply. With some systems, the drip tubes all work completely independently of one another so that plants with different requirements can receive the correct amount of water. The system may either be connected to the water supply via a pressure reducer, or water for it may be drawn from a high-level tank. Yet another variant enables you to specify the intervals between waterings and the duration of each watering using a computer. It is important to take an expert's advice when buying any such system, and whatever you choose should be tested for at least a month to make sure that all is working as it should.

## Why should you feed plants?

Plants need many nutrients if they are to make healthy growth, and they can only absorb these nutrients in soluble form. Normally in the soil, the organic constituents of micro-organisms are gradually broken down and converted into mineral form. They are then ready to be taken up by plants. This process is called mineralization. Container plants have to produce a large quantity of flowers but their roots only have access to a very limited volume of compost, so the nutrients available from this natural process are not sufficient. The plants have to be supplied on a regular basis with an 'artificial' feed in the form of a mineral or organic fertilizer.

In the portrait sections you will find information about the nutrient requirements of each plant. A plant's needs vary during its life cycle from the average amounts stated, with the young plant not requiring such large quantities of nutrients as the fully grown patio plant that has a large mass of leaves and flowers to keep

*Some of the different kinds of fertilizers available.*

supplied. The conditions under which a plant grows, such as the amount of light and warmth it receives, also affect its need for nutrients. An experienced gardener with the proverbial 'green fingers' observes his plants' growth, considers these factors and tries to adapt his applications of fertilizer as far as possible to the needs of the moment. The plants will be at their most vigorous when they are neither underfed nor overfed. When talking about fertilizers, a differentiation must be made between base fertilizer and subsequent applications of fertilizer.

### Base fertilizer as a constituent of composts

Composts should contain a base fertilizer so that freshly planted flowers will have a sufficient supply of nutrients right from the start. This is normally a slow-release fertilizer.

**Composts:** the ready-made composts, among them those made to the John Innes specifications, have already had a base fertilizer in the form of a slow-release fertilizer added to them, and so can be put straight to use. How long the slow-release fertilizer will continue to work is shown on the bag. Some composts contain fertilizer that will last for 3-4 months, but normally there is only sufficient for the first 6-8 weeks after planting. After this time, you **must** start to give subsequent applications of fertilizer.

## Subsequent applications of fertilizer

You should not forget to give subsequent applications of fertilizer at the right time!

When the balcony plants, with their needs supplied by the base fertilizer, are flowering beautifully during their first flowering period, it is easy to forget to give a subsequent application of fertilizer. The plants then start to suffer from deficiencies and will fail to produce further blooms. This means that you will experience the dreaded gap between one set of plants finishing flowering and the next set coming into bloom. If you want to avoid this, you will have to be ready on time with your applications of fertilizer.

## Methods of applying fertilizer

### 1. Scattering on a slow-release fertilizer

The simplest but also the most expensive way to make subsequent applications of fertilizer is to scatter a slow-release fertilizer on to the compost. This method is only appropriate if you water the boxes by hand from above so that the fertilizer can be dissolved. Depending on the duration of effect of the fertilizer, a maximum of two applications will be necessary. For the amateur gardener there are long-term fertilizers in the form of **plant food spikes** that you simply push into the compost. The packaging will give information on the number of sticks required and their duration of effect. For plants with a moderate nutrient requirement, at least 20 sticks will be needed for a standard-sized window box 20 cm (8 inches) wide.

### 2. Weekly liquid feeds

Container flowers are usually fed with a liquid feed once a week. Use a complete fertilizer for this purpose that is high in phosphates. You will find such fertilizers sold as being suitable for flowering plants.

A purely organic fertilizer that is high in phosphates is 'Peru guano flower fertilizer'. The usual recommendation is to add it weekly to a watering can full of water in a concentration of two parts per thousand. This amount corresponds approximately to the average needs of plants that require a low or moderate amount of nutrients. However, it is not enough for flowers with a high nutrient requirement. This must be the reason why many plants often look half-starved, for the low doses of fertilizer given make little allowance for the vigour and potential flowering ability of these summer flowers.

### 3. Liquid feeds with every watering

Plants react to excess in exactly the same way as people. If you are made to consume an entire day's or even week's food at one meal, you end up with a stomach ache and after a day you feel very hungry again. Plants, too, need their 'meals' to be spread out, so it is advisable to give them less fertilizer but more often. The best and surest method of getting vigorous summer plants that flower non-stop is to give a low-concentration feed, suited to the plants' requirements, at each watering. Do not give the required quantity of fertilizer all at once, but divide it into smaller doses over the course of the week. In that way the plants will not get 'stomach ache' and will only 'eat' as much as they can take. This method also ensures that the quantities of fertilizer are automatically adapted to the weather conditions and conditions on the patio or balcony. In good weather the leaves lose a lot of water through evaporation and therefore need a greater quantity of nutrients. Because watering is increased on hot days, the flowers are also given correspondingly more nutrients. In bad weather watering is decreased and the plants automatically get less fertilizer.

## How to measure low doses of fertilizer

In the case of plants requiring a small amount of nutrients, dissolve a heaped teaspoonful (about 5 ml) in a can of water (10 litres or 2 gallons). Plants requiring a moderate amount of nutrients need 1-2 teaspoonfuls (about 5-10 ml) in a can of water (10 litres or 2 gallons), and those requiring a high amount of nutrients need 2-3 teaspoonfuls (about 10-15 ml) dissolved in a can of water (10 litres or 2 gallons).

**Important:** Stir vigorously to ensure that the fertilizer is properly dissolved. Proceed in a similar manner for liquid fertilizer, but in this case use the bottle cap as a measure (read the instructions carefully). If you have a 5 ml (1 teaspoon) cap as a measure, use one cap of liquid fertilizer to 10 litres (2 gallons) of water for plants with a low nutrient requirement, two caps for those with a moderate nutrient requirement and so on. The best way to administer fertilizer is via an automatic watering system that premixes the feed and distributes it to the micro-drip tubes. Once installed and adjusted, you will not have to worry about it any more all summer long.

When using a ready-mixed compost with a base fertilizer, do not add any fertilizer at first when watering. Only after 6-8 weeks do you need to start feeding the plants. You can then expect that watering will occur on average six times per week and set the machine to 0.5 or 1.0 parts per thousand.

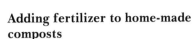

### Adding fertilizer to home-made composts

If you are using a standard compost, the nutrients are available in balanced proportions. If you make your own mixture with garden compost, the plants may exhibit signs of deficiency due to an excess or lack of a main or trace element. The plants may not grow well or they may develop chlorotic yellow leaves or reddish leaves. To overcome this, you should send a sample of your compost to a laboratory. In return you will receive information about the nutrient content and also a recommendation on what fertilizer to use. Generally, garden compost has a very high phosphorus and potash content, a lot of lime and very little nitrogen. Trace elements are present in balanced proportions. The very high proportion of lime can be a problem because it can increase the pH to such an extent that iron is no longer available to the plants. They quickly react by developing yellow leaves, but these can soon be restored to normal by giving the plants a special soil acidifier plant food that contains iron and other trace elements.

### Base fertilizer

Since garden compost is very rich in nutrients, it must be considered to be an organic fertilizer in its own right, because only nitrogen is missing. For this reason, when mixing your own potting compost, you should add an organic nitrogen fertilizer in the form of hoof and horn meal.
Use 4-6 kg/cubic metre (4-6 oz/cubic foot) of compost, depending on the result of the laboratory analysis.

### Subsequent applications of fertilizer

For plants with a low nutrient requirement, this supply of nutrients is generally sufficient. Plants with a moderate or high nutrient requirement need regular subsequent applications of fertilizer after 4-6 weeks.

For this purpose, it is best to use a complete fertilizer that is a soil acidifier and has a high nitrogen content.

## The correct choice of woody plants

Make sure when selecting your plants that only those with similar requirements are planted together. Woody plants can be divided into two groups:

1. lime-loving trees and shrubs
2. acid-loving trees and shrubs

Only plants that belong to the same group should be combined. The container should also be appropriate to the plants' growth habit. It is best to seek advice about this from the nursery. When choosing plants, look carefully at the root ball. Healthy roots always have white tips.

*The plants in the tub all like acid soil.*

## Choosing the correct compost for permanent planting

In contrast to the plants in seasonal planting schemes, woody plants and herbaceous perennials remain in the same container for many years without a change of compost. In order to maintain a high degree of structural stability over a long period, composts should have at least 30-40% mineral material mixed in with them. The best materials have proved to be expanded clay or brick rubble. Basically, only those plants should be planted together in a container that tolerate the same soil pH range. Apart from lime-loving plants which require an alkaline soil, there are those that need an acid soil. Conifers and wild herbaceous perennials require compost with a low nutrient content. Deciduous trees and shrubs and showpiece herbaceous perennials require compost with a moderate nutrient content.

# Planting trees and shrubs in containers and boxes

Woody plants and herbaceous perennials are mostly sold in pots or containers and can be planted at any time of year. The only time when you cannot plant them is if the compost is frozen.

Deciduous trees, shrubs and roses are also sold more cheaply bare-rooted, as are conifers that simply have a root ball. These are best planted in early spring.

Experience has shown that woody plants planted in the spring become established more quickly and are well prepared for the coming winter. If you have missed the spring planting time, there is still a chance to plant in autumn.

## Insulating containers against frost

The roots are the parts of a plant that are most liable to frost damage. If winters are cold in your area, you should **always** insulate the root ball when setting plants in pots. Cut to size a sheet of plastic bubble wrap and line the inside of your container or window box so that there are no gaps left uncovered. At the bottom of the container, arrange a 5 cm (2 inch) deep layer of expanded clay to provide insulation and soak up water. Containers prepared in this way do not need to be protected from the outside with ugly sheets of plastic bubble wrap.

**Drainage** without exception, all trees and shrubs, including those that like acid soil, will not tolerate waterlogging. For this reason, excess water must be able to flow quickly out of the container. Important: every container should have adequate drainage holes in the base. You will sometimes have to drill or expand these yourself. To prevent the holes from becoming blocked, cover them with pieces of broken flowerpot. You will then need a drainage layer of expanded clay measuring 3 cm (1$^1$/2 inches) deep in a box and 5-10 cm (2-4 inches) in a container.

**Filter layer:** to prevent compost from being washed into the drainage layer and blocking it, line the entire container with fibre fleece so that the ends hang over the edge. Trim the ends only after the container has been filled with compost.

**Filling with compost:** once you have prepared the container in this way, you can fill it with compost. Press the compost down lightly from time to time as you fill so that the level will not drop as it settles. You should not position the plant too high, but should leave a sufficient gap between the compost and the top of the container to facilitate watering.

**Planting:** plants sold in pots must of course be taken out of their pots before planting. Inside the pot, the roots will have twined themselves around the root ball and you will need to loosen them. Now place all the plants in the container of compost. They are at the right height if the tops of the root balls are about 2 cm (1 inch) below the edge of the container. Now you can fill in the gaps all round with compost, remembering to leave a space for watering.

**Bare-rooted plants:** the roots should be soaked in a container of water for 2-3 hours before planting. Trim the roots a little first, so that they can soak up the water more easily.

**Watering in:** finally, water the plants thoroughly. Keep on watering until the water comes out of the drainage holes. This ensures that the deepest layers of compost are also well moistened.

*Important:* If the container is standing on the floor, you must make sure that the drainage hole is not blocked. To prevent this, stand containers on strips of wood 1-2 cm ($^1$/2-1 inch) thick.

# Feeding permanent planting subjects

Long-lived plants requiring a low (conifers, wild herbaceous perennials) or moderate (deciduous trees and shrubs, showpiece herbaceous perennials) amount of nutrients do not need very much fertilizer. For this reason, they are either fed using a slow-release fertilizer or an organic fertilizer that provides a store of nutrients.

To treat acute nutrient defiencies (recognizable by the older leaves becoming lighter in colour), use a short-acting fertilizer with an NPK ratio of 15:11:17.

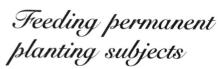

*Effective root ball protection prevents frost damage: plastic bubble wrap.*

Evergreen woody plants need larger amounts of magnesium. If the plants develop yellow colorations to their needles or leaves, you will need to give them a potash and magnesium feed as well. (Look for conifer fertilizer at your garden centre.)

## Further points on feeding woody plants

### 1. When using standard compost
An ideal fertilizer for woody plants is Osmocote plus. Osmocote plus works for 6 months after the tablets have been pushed into the compost in early spring. The clumps of granules dissolve slowly and the nutrients are transported to the plants' roots each time they are watered. If you are using powdered fertilizer, none should be allowed to remain on the leaves. As an alternative, you could use the practical plant food spikes that you simply push into the compost.

*Applying subsequent fertilizer during the year of planting*
Manufactured composts already contain a base fertilizer. You only need to apply fertilizer after the base fertilizer ceases to be effective (read the information on the compost bag). Normally, a single subsequent application of a shorter-acting controlled-release fertilizer is sufficient.

*Subsequent applications of fertilizer during the second year*
In the years that follow, you would do best to feed your plants with a slow-release fertilizer that is specially formulated for trees and shrubs. An exceptionally slow-dissolving nine-month form is particularly recommended. One application in early spring is then sufficient.

### 2. Home-made composts
Above all with 'live' composts such as home-made composts with a high proportion of garden compost, complete organic and mineral fertilizers provide a good supply of nutrients for woody plants.

*Subsequent applications of fertilizer in the planting year*
Compost made from well-rotted material mostly contains many nutrients with the exception of nitrogen and these are sufficient for the first year of the tree's or shrub's growth. You only need to make up for the nitrogen deficiency with hoof and horn meal. Too high a pH can lead to chlorotic yellow leaves. Mostly this is due to iron difficiency so, as a prophylactic measure, apply a soil acidifier plant food.

*Subsequent applications of fertilizer in the second year*
If you want to continue growing your plants organically, you should use guano in solid form. All other organic complete fertilizers are combinations of organic and mineral substances to which has been added potash in the form of a salt that is immediately water-soluble. For woody plants, a fertilizer with an NPK ratio of 7:3:7 is particularly suitable because of its relatively low phosphorus content. All organic fertilizers must be worked into the compost or covered with a 2-3 cm (good inch) layer of growing medium because the release of nutrients by micro-organisms is dependent on moisture.
***Tip:*** empty your teapot regularly on to alkaline soil. The high tannin content will lower the pH value.

# Watering trees and shrubs correctly

Woody plants are also very modest in their water requirements. Nevertheless, you should water their containers regularly both summer and winter. Evergreens especially lose water through evaporation when it is frosty in winter and must be watered regularly on frost-free days. Following a dry autumn, evergreens should be given a thorough watering at the end of November.

# Protecting bulbs and herbaceous perennials from frost

If you want to plant bulbs yourself, the best time to do so is in September. The widest choice is available in autumnn, and the bulbs will have plenty of time to grow roots. To enable the frost-tender bulbs to survive the winter, the boxes must be prevented from freezing through. There are three ways to do this:

### 1. Protecting from frost on the patio
It is possible to insulate both the inside and outside of container walls. Plastic bubble wrap and polystyrene shapes, used to fill the space between an outer an inner container, are suitable materials.

*The box within a box method protects against frost.*

The base of the planted container is lined with a 3-5 cm (1½-2 inch) deep layer of expanded clay. The clay is porous and serves both as drainage and as insulation.

Place a piece of fibre fleece above this layer, then fill up with compost and bulbs. The fibre fleece separates the two layers, preventing the compost from becoming mixed with the expanded clay so that the latter can be used over and over again.

On top of the box you can then make an airy covering of fir branches. If there is enough space, you could push the ends of the branches carefully between the wall of the box and the compost. Be sure to remove the covering in good time in spring.

### 2. Storing indoors

Herbaceous perennials and bulbs can be successfully kept in a cold shed, garage, underground garage or cellar during the winter.

### 3. Protecting from frost in the garden

Sink the ready-planted container into the soil right up to the rim and cover with fir branches.

*Important:* Even in winter the boxes should be checked to make sure that they are not dry, whether in the garden, on the patio or in the house. If the compost feels dry, water carefully on a frost-free day.

*Tip:* if you use a 20 cm (8 inch) wide box for summer flowers, use a 15 cm (6 inch) wide box for bulbs. When planted with spring bulbs, this can then simply be placed inside the larger box and the gap between the boxes filled with insulating material.

# Designing a seasonal balcony

Before you start planting, you should be clear about how the balcony will be used. If your balcony is to be first and foremost a decorative feature of your house, you should hang the boxes on the outside of the railings and plant magnificent balcony flowers that can easily be seen from a distance. Boxes hung on the outside have the advantage that you will still have plenty of space in which to sit on the balcony. However, if you are one of those people who think of their balcony as a substitute for a garden, you should hang the box on the inside of the railings.

## Designing mixed boxes

Compared with boxes devoted to one species, colourful mixed plantings consisting of various species of flower require more precise knowledge about the growth habits of the individual plants. Also, the enormous range of colours can be quite bewildering, so you need a good sense of colour in order to create harmonious combinations.

You should not leave colour schemes to chance, for it is all too easy to get into a real muddle. So decide on this year's colour scheme before you even think about buying the plants. This will make it easier when you come to make your choice from the enormous range of plants on offer. If you are buying plants from a nursery, it is advisable to plant your boxes then and there. The finished boxes can then be hung straight on the balcony railings, and there will be no big mess to clear up afterwards.

# Colour combinations

## Combining two complementary colours

If you like combining contrasting colours, plant complementary colours next to each other. Complementary colours are those that are found opposite each other on the colour wheel. The classic pairs of colours are yellow/purple, blue/orange, red/green. These colours have an intensifying effect on one another and produce the greatest brilliance (see pages 103, 189).

## Combining three colours

If you like strong colours, you could plant a combination of the pure primary colours yellow, red and blue such as the painter Mondrian uses (see pages 36, 102). If these colours are too gaudy for your liking, plant a combination of three pastel shades (see page 103).

## Gradations of colour

Lovers of delicate colours could plant flowers that bloom in many shades of their favourite colour. To avoid such a scheme becoming monotonous, you should not stick doggedly to one colour. Either combine the warm colours yellow/red/orange or the cool colours blue/purple/green, and make use of the psychological effect of the colours. Warm colours have a stimulating effect and also make an area appear smaller, while cool colours have a calming effect and make the display look bigger.

Any colour combination will be enhanced by an interplanting of foliage plants.

## Patio or balcony layout

If several boxes are to be planted for the setting, you need to ensure that they will go together to make a harmonious whole. It makes no sense to plant each of the boxes separately. If you are able to plant them at the nursery, number the boxes according to their position on the balcony. Then proceed as follows: begin by distributing the dominant plants throughout all the boxes. This gives a basic framework around which you can position the subordinate plants. Only choose plants that go well together from the point of view of type and requirements (e.g. plants with delicate foliage are soon over-grown by plants with large leaves). Think of a pattern for arranging your plants and create variations on a

theme by putting together a group of plants, then repeating the group, altering the sequence slightly each time. Use restful green foliage plants interspersed among the combinations of colours to provide a 'break' from the brilliant display. To make an even more interesting design, plants of striking appearance can be used here and there to give emphasis. Such plants are the optical equivalent of a drum beat and should of course be used sparingly.

### Container plants

Vigorous container plants (e.g. *Datura*), particularly if they are bush-shaped, soon take up too much space on a small area. It is better to do without such plants and instead choose standards (with stems at least 1.50 metres or 5 feet high) and climbing plants trained up supports (see section on climbing plants).

*These complementary colours have an intensifying effect on each other and produce great brilliance.*

Place standards where they will be sheltered from the wind, or tie them to supports, otherwise they will be blown over repeatedly.

### How to make a small area look bigger

A rear wall of mirrors will make a small design look twice the size. The predominant use of blues and purples in the colour scheme will also make a setting look larger.

## Patio or balcony layout

If several boxes are to be planted for the setting, you need to ensure that they will go together to make a harmonious whole. It makes no sense to plant each of the boxes separately. If you are able to plant them at the nursery, number the boxes according to their position on the balcony. Then proceed as follows: begin by distributing the dominant plants throughout all the boxes. This gives a basic framework around which you can position the subordinate plants. Only choose plants that go well together from the point of view of type and requirements (e.g. plants with delicate foliage are soon over-grown by plants with large leaves). Think of a pattern for arranging your plants and create variations on a

theme by putting together a group of plants, then repeating the group, altering the sequence slightly each time. Use restful green foliage plants interspersed among the combinations of colours to provide a 'break' from the brilliant display. To make an even more interesting design, plants of striking appearance can be used here and there to give emphasis. Such plants are the optical equivalent of a drum beat and should of course be used sparingly.

### Container plants

Vigorous container plants (e.g. *Datura*), particularly if they are bush-shaped, soon take up too much space on a small area. It is better to do without such plants and instead choose standards (with stems at least 1.50 metres or 5 feet high) and climbing plants trained up supports (see section on climbing plants).

*These complementary colours have an intensifying effect on each other and produce great brilliance.*

Place standards where they will be sheltered from the wind, or tie them to supports, otherwise they will be blown over repeatedly.

### How to make a small area look bigger

A rear wall of mirrors will make a small design look twice the size. The predominant use of blues and purples in the colour scheme will also make a setting look larger.

Translated from the German by Lilian Hall
in association with First EditionTranslations Ltd, Cambridge, U.K.

Photography: Friedrich Strauß
Editorial: Barbara Kiesewetter
Layout: Anton Walter


ACKNOWLEDGMENTS

The authors would like to thank Herr Alois Reis, master horticulturalist at the
Institut für Freiraumpflanzung, FH Weihenstephan for his invaluable specialist advice.

For assistance with the illustrations we would like to thank:

Institut für Zierpflanzenbau
der FH Weihenstephan

Fa. Kientzler Jungpflanzen
Postfach 100
55457 Gensingen

Fischer Baumschule
85775 Fahrenzhausen-Bärnau

Gartenbau Wolf
Holzbrünnistraße 17
85410 Haag an der Amper

Ernst Benary Samenzucht GmbH
34346 Hann. Münden

Fa. Pelargonien Fischer
54426 Hillscheid